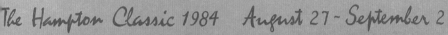

The Hampton Classic 1984   August 27 ~ September 2

Hampton Classic Horse Show

SNAKE HOLLOW ROAD, BRIDGEHAMPTON, NEW YORK

August 26 ~ September 1, 1985

The 1988 HAMPTON CLASSIC · JULY 24-31

SNAKE HOLLOW ROAD, BRIDGEHAMPTON, NEW YORK

THE HAMPTON CLASSIC
AUG. 24 ~ AUG. 31, 1986

THE CLASSIC EXPERIENCE

THE CLASSIC EXPERIENCE

The Hampton Classic
Bridgehampton, N.Y.

BRYANT CARPENTER • PHOTOS BY HELEN CARPENTER

CARL MILLER, PUBLISHER

AMERICAN YEARBOOK SALES, INC.

PRINTED IN U.S.A.
JOSTENS PRINTING & PUBLISHING

ENDSHEETS
Images of posters designed annually, celebrating
America's largest outdoor horse show.
Posters loaned by The Hampton Classic Horse Show.

COVER
Rider *Kate Chope* on *Hearsay* owned by *Kate Chope*

TITLE
The Classic Experience, an all-encompassing title depicting
The Hampton Classic, was recommended by
Diana De Rosa, Press Officer,
The Hampton Classic Horse Show.

FIRST EDITION
1995

LIBRARY OF CONGRESS CATALOGING-IN-PUBLICATION DATA
Library of Congress Catalog Card Number 94-73560

CARPENTER, BRYANT
The Classic Experience, The Hampton Classic, Bridgehampton, New York
with Carl W. Miller: Additional photographs by Helen Carpenter

ISBN: 0-9645332-0-0
includes bibliographical references

1.Horse Show Competition, New York. 2.Celebrities 3.The Hamptons, New York 4.Social Life and Customs

10 9 8 7 6 5 4 3 2 1

Designed and Published By
Carl W. Miller
Carl Miller American Yearbook Sales, Inc.
516-751-1712

Printed in U.S.A.

Jostens Printing & Publishing

Contents

Introduction

The Hampton Classic. For beauty, prestige and pure size, it is unparalleled on the outdoor show riding circuit. Since making its debut in 1976, it has become the largest outdoor horse show in America, and one of the most revered.

Each year, in late summer, the pageant plays in Bridgehampton, New York. Each year more than one thousand riders come to perform, more than one thousand horses. Children and amateurs ride; pros chase a $100,000 purse in the Grand Prix ring.

But the Classic is more than riders and horses and ribbons. It is a major social event on New York's ritziest summer stage, the Hamptons. Celebrities, entertainers, movie stars, millionaires and big-name sponsors are among the 40,000 who make the annual pilgrimage to the Classic.

No other outdoor horse show in America draws such a crowd. No other show draws such media attention. No other show becomes so entwined with the surrounding community, or features so many special events.

The Classic is truly a show of many dimensions. It is a show whose roots trace back to the turn of the century. It is a show that has been led to the top by people who, when they started, had little to no experience running equestrian events. It is a show that draws huge corporate sponsorship and top-name professional riders all while remaining, at its heart, a show that is a local event. It is a benefit for nearby Southampton Hospital, as well as other beneficiaries.

The Classic rides but one week of the year. This book, The Classic Experience, aims to make the Hampton Classic a memory that can be relived in any season, long after the show tents come down for the year. Released just before the Classic's 20th anniversary, The Classic Experience details the history of the show and tells the story of the players, the riding, the hoopla, the locals, the behind the scenes people and all the other elements that combine to make the show what it is: The best.

The concept of an illustrated narrative on the Hampton Classic was initiated by Publisher/Designer Carl W. Miller. It was written, laid out, and in spots, photographed by Bryant Carpenter, sports editor of the Southampton Press, a weekly newspaper in the Hamptons. Much of the photography, including the cover shot, was provided by Mr. Carpenter's wife, Helen B. Carpenter.

Read on and enjoy the ride ...

JUMP FLOWERS COURTESY
FIVE TRAILS FARM

HAMPTONS CLASSIC

INCORPORATING THE SOUTHAMPTON HORSE SHOW / FOR THE BENEFIT OF SOUTHAMPTON HOSPITAL

AUG. 29-SEPT. 2, 1978

GREEN HOLLOW ROAD & MONTAUK HIGHWAY, EAST HAMPTON, NEW YORK

Chapter I: Classic History

You don't become one of the country's largest and richest outdoor horse shows overnight. Nothing that big ever comes easy. You have to stand the test of time, the test of human events, the test of personalities, even the test of Mother Nature. Throughout its history, the Hampton Classic and the shows to which its origins can be traced have, despite some failures, passed the tests well enough to not only survive, but to thrive.

The Classic as we more or less now know it began in 1976, though it wouldn't take the name "The Hampton Classic" for another year. The roots, however, burrow much deeper than that. They trace, in fact, all the way back to the turn of the 20th century. There, at the base of the Hampton Classic family tree, stands an annual event that was known simply as the Horse Show. It was held in Southampton on open fields off First Neck Lane that overlooked Agawam Lake.

This little equestrian get-together, more of a social gathering than a real sports event, carried on every year until the outbreak of World War I. The harsh reality of a world at war stopped the show altogether. It would return in the 1920's, galloping back on the shoulders of a newly formed group called the Southampton Riding and Hunt Club. The club based its headquarters just to the north of Southampton Village on property along Majors Path. The club was, you could say, meticulous. It took six years to complete work on club barns and stables. But it was worth the wait. When the facilities were unveiled in 1928 they were ranked among the best in the East.

The Twenties roared. In the Hamptons, they also neighed. With the rise of the Southampton Riding and Hunt Club came the return of the Horse Show. Still maintaining its social dimensions, the show was largely a nice day in the country for wealthy folks. Despite the specter of the Great Depression, it was held every summer through the 1930's.

The coming of the Second World War brought an end to the fun and games. On top of that, the club founder died. The club broke up altogether, selling its horses and stables. Aside from a two-year stint in the late 1950's, the role of the Majors Path farm as home to the prize horse show of the Hamptons was over.

The war overseas came to an end, and a new world order divided along East-West ideological lines emerged. On a more limited front out here, the Horse Show re-emerged as well, and it too was steadily reshaped. Initially, after lying dormant throughout the 1940's, the Horse Show made its comeback in the 1950's. But it wasn't the same. The show simply lacked the pageantry and popularity of the Golden Years.

Then, in 1959, there was a breakthrough. The Soviet Union and U.S. were putting unmanned craft into space. In Southampton, Mrs. Morris Scott Wadley picked up the organizational reins and made the Horse Show a fundraiser for the Parrish Art Museum. This show was held at the Stanley Howard Estate in North Sea. It was also formally incorporated as the Southampton Horse Show. Also important, the show regained its former glamour and, in a tradition that remains until this day, it became a major summer social event.

Apparently, though, the show couldn't take too much of a good thing. Reflecting a decade that would be turbulent across America, Southampton Horse Show board members argued amongst themselves. Disputes spilled into court. Turned off, the Parrish Art Museum formally broke away from the show in 1964. For a while, the show was inactive. The tradition, it seemed, was over. Long Island, like the rest of the country, focused its attention on the greater upheavals of the day: Vietnam, civil rights, assassination.

Despite the disappearance of the Southampton Horse Show, riding remained popular in the Hamptons. By 1970, several horse farms were established on the East End, including Stony Hill Stables, the Topping Riding Club and Swan Creek Farms - farms that all exist to this day. These farms offered lessons and held small, unrecognized shows. They were also the first ripple of an equestrian wave that would steadily crest across the Hamptons over the next 25 years.

Rising hand-in-hand with this phenomenon was the revival of the Southampton Horse Show. The old shows were still a fresh memory. The loss of a Hamptons tradition - seven years had passed without a show - seemed a sad waste.

Lolly Clarke riding Summer Song at the 1966 Southampton Horse Show in North Sea. Clarke and Summer Song were Junior Hunter Champions that year. The show would be one of the last for the Southampton Horse Show before it was resurrected through the Sagaponack Horse Show at Topping Riding Club. Photo courtesy of Lolly Clark.

Thus it was that the Southampton Horse Show made its return in 1971 under the lead of Diana Schwenk, who held the show's charter with the American Horse Show Association. The resurrection was made through another show. That show was the Sagaponack Horse Show. For several years, Bud and Tinka Topping had been hosting the event at their Topping Riding Club as a benefit for the Hampton Day School. When Schwenk suggested the old Southampton Horse Show be revived through the Topping event, Bud and Tinka went along. For the next few years they would host the newly established Southampton Horse Show.

The show would quickly outgrow its borders. The greatest change was one generated by the sport of show riding itself. For a long time, horse shows were synonymous with social gatherings.

They really weren't considered sporting events. That began to change in the 60's and 70's when training and judging came into play. The competition improved. Wishing to bring such a show closer to home, Marie-Christophe de Menil of Sag Harbor suggested in 1976 that the Southampton Horse Show, for all its history a society-based, one-day local event, be upgraded to A-rated status. This meant a larger, multi-day show. It meant a better one, too. With an A-rating, the show would feature jumping, and that was sure to attract the top riders and horses.

This was a big step up, the one that directly spawned the modern day Hampton Classic. Some major changes were necessary to get it there. For starters, a bigger show needed bigger grounds. Thus, the show moved from Topping Riding over to Dune Alpin Farm in East Hampton.

"Waiting at the In-Gate" Photo courtesy of The Hampton Classic

Preparations for the first A-rated show in the Hamptons proceeded nicely. Tents and stables went up, horses started to arrive. Everything was going according to plan ... until Belle showed up. Hurricane Belle, that is. On the eve of the show the storm came barreling through. The place was levelled. Tents and stables, everything came down. Horses had to be evacuated.

Still, as the saying goes, the show must go on, and it did. Thanks to Herculean efforts by work crews, the new A-rated Southampton Horse Show opened a little more than a day behind schedule. (Incidentally, the caterers at the first show were a couple by the name of Anthony Hitchcock and Jean Lindgren. In six years, they would become the executive directors of the Hampton Classic.)

The Hampton Classic would be remembered for its stormy baptism. It established tradition. In years to come, other Classics would share a similar fate with savage weather.

Despite the stormy start, the show's future steadily brightened. In 1977, the show officially became known as the Hampton Classic. The name change was generated by two factors. One, the show was organized and attended by people from across the East End of Long Island. A regional title was clearly

A Stormy Tradition

The Hampton Classic is no stranger to bad weather. Not just bad weather, but extreme, nasty, violent, untimely weather.

Mother Nature dealt the Classic a mean blow in its maiden year as an A-rated show. In subsequent years she has intermittently recalled the Classic to the sting of her hand. She's dealt hurricanes. She's dealt tornadoes. She's dealt rains so heavy an ark would have been of more use than a stable.

It must be fate - some sort of periodic test of the Classic's mettle - because the meteorological trend was established on Day 1. That was August 12, 1976. It was the very night before the show's A-rated debut. Everything was set up at Dune Alpin Farm, the East Hampton property where the show was being held. All the horses were in. All the rings were ready for riding. Then the storm came. It was Hurricane Belle, and she bestowed upon the show a wet and windy baptism.

Actually, it could have been worse. Early reports had the storm's eye passing right over Southampton - at high tide, no less. Anxious residents tracking the storm feared a repeat of the destructive Hurricane Carol of 1954. Fortunately, the storm wasn't that bad. As she approached Long Island, Belle weakened and veered a bit to the west, casting her eye over Nassau County instead.

Still, the grounds at Dune Alpin were in disarray. The tents and temporary stables were all blown down. Horses had been evacuated, many to local barns. Getting the show off, at that point, must have seemed hopeless. But it wasn't. Work crews tackled the mess non-stop. They were so energetic that the show started only a day and a half behind schedule. Thus was established another Classic tradition: An ability to persevere in trying circumstances.

In 1982, the Classic moved from Dune Alpin to its current home off Snake Hollow Road in Bridgehampton. The relocation did not change the show's luck with the weather. Like the person terrorized even after moving out of the haunted house, the Classic was hounded by the weather gremlins. They came in tornado form and tore apart tents and stables. Fortunately, the Classic had a week to regroup. Replacement equipment was flown in and the show, naturally, went on.

Then came 1985, the infamous "Year of the Mud." Conditions were so bad they warranted a title. Torrential rains fell just before the start of the show, leaving the grounds oozing with mud. It was knee-deep in places and the Classic was simply not prepared to deal with it. The parking lot was out of commission; cars and trucks became mired. In the rings, it was tough going for horse and rider. Spectators had no hope of keeping their shoes clean as they squished about.

The weather cleared and the place did dry out some, but that didn't do much for the smell. "The stench here was unbearable," recalled Classic landscaper Miki Gilsenan, "just like rotten spuds."

To make matters worse, Mother Nature packed a one-two punch. Just before the second weekend she unleashed another rain-heavy roundhouse. This storm was vicious. Tornadoes touched down across the South Fork. They missed the Classic, but the grounds were a veritable bayou from the rain. New rivers and lakes had taken form. Pumps had to be brought in to clear the water. It was sent down a stream that cut through a Hunter ring and emptied into Long Pond down beyond the parking lot. It was a mess. But in keeping with that Classic tradition of finding silver linings amid dark clouds, the weather was perfect for Grand Prix Sunday and a record crowd filled the stands.

The 1985 nightmare had another positive upshot: It taught the Classic a lesson. Physical improvements were made to the grounds. Roads were stabilized, drains were laid. As a result, the Classic was better prepared to deal with the nasty rains that fell upon the show in 1987, 1988 and 1990.

Obviously, improvements to the grounds can offer only so much protection. If it rains hard during show hours there is nothing the Classic can do but postpone for the day. Such was the case in 1990, when one particularly bad day of rain wiped out an entire slate of events. Pumps were brought in to make the place passable for the rest of the week. Still, a whole day had been irretrievably lost.

Ironically, the show has been fairly lucky with the weather in the 90's. In 1991, Hurricane Bob splashed through. It wasn't a pleasant experience for the East End, but at least the timing was good, as far as the Classic went. (Bob came two weeks before the show.) There were hurricane watches in 1992 and 1993, but they did not pan out. Instead, the Classic was left with sensational weather. The same was true in 1994. Sure, Grand Prix Sunday was cool and cloudy, but the rest of the week was idyllic. The only day of rain was Monday, which never features riding anyway.

Talk about perfect timing. Could it be a new trend? Could an old jinx be broken? Shhh, keep your voice down. She'll hear you.

Bud Topping & Bigfoot. Photo courtesy of Neil O'Connor

in order. Second, it was a bit incongruous to have a show held in East Hampton run under a Southampton title. The Hampton Classic was the result.

1977 was also the year the show was established as a benefit for Southampton Hospital, a tradition that has continued since. Back then, when the outlook was uncertain, Marie-Christophe de Menil underwrote the show and personally guaranteed the hospital a donation if the show operated at a loss.

The show grew. It drew more riders, more horses. Several local riders such as Jenno Topping were doing well on the national circuit, and that helped bring in the fans. A bigger show went hand-in-hand with bigger organization. In the early 80's, Agneta Currey assumed the chairmanship of the show. Hitchcock and Lindgren became executive directors. These people, along with an ambitious Board of Directors, guided the show from a mere local affair to one of the country's biggest.

There were boosts along the way: big sponsorships, increased status in the equestrian world. In 1981, a watershed year, the Classic became a benefit for the U.S. Equestrian Team. Not only did that improve the standards of the show, it also made the Classic Grand Prix one of the qualifying events for the World Cup.

Like any thriving organism, the Hampton Classic remained in growing flux. In 1982, the show was moved to its present location on Snake Hollow Road in Bridgehampton. The move provided the physical space - 60 acres, in all - that has allowed the Classic to become the nation's largest outdoor horse show. As for duration, in 1984 the Classic expanded from five days to seven. As an improvement on that, in 1986 the show moved Opening Day to a Sunday. That allowed the show to play on two consecutive week-

ends, culminating on the second Sunday with the Grand Prix. The exposure grew. In 1987, ESPN paid a visit. For the first time, the Hampton Classic was televised, and TV meant more prestige, more exposure not only for the show, but for sponsors.

Logistics continued to shift. In 1988, the show temporarily abandoned its traditional late August dates for the latter part of July. This was done so American horses could meet quarantine requirements for the Olympics, which were held that year in Seoul, South Korea. Three years later, the show reverted back to its traditional pre-Labor Day schedule.

And so the show went on, even in dark hours. From time to time, Mother Nature dealt a mean blow. In 1982, a tornado baptized the Classic's relocation to Bridgehampton. Tents and stables were destroyed. Fortunately, the show was still a week or so away, which gave plenty of time for new equipment to be

Grand Prix riding at the 1983 Hampton Classic. Photo courtesy of The Hampton Classic

1983 Grand Prix crowd.   Note the hay bales and rudimentary bleachers - a far cry from today's accommodations.
Photo courtesy of The Hampton Classic

Profile: Tinka Topping

Tinka Topping remembers the early shows. Like a mother, she remembers the fitful, exciting days when an infant Hampton Classic cut its teeth in the eye of a storm, when a cub Classic struggled for attention.

Topping was one of the people who ushered in the Classic when it became an A-rated show in 1976. She is a Classic parent. And like a good parent, she helped the Classic grow from an underling to a model show.

Topping was actually mothering the Classic before it was the Classic. For several years in the early 1970's, she and husband Bud hosted the Classic's forerunner, the Southampton Horse Show, at their Sagaponack farm, Topping Riding Club. When the show stepped up to an A rating and packed its bags for the more spacious fields of Dune Alpin Farm in East Hampton, Tinka followed.

In that first year, organizers were a little out of their element. Sure, they had run shows before, but not one this big or this involved.

"I was the show secretary and I didn't even have a clue," Tinka recalled with a chuckle. "We had walkie-talkies and they didn't even work. We had all this machinery and didn't know how to use it."

It was hard enough being figuratively wet behind the ears. But how about being literally soaked? The arrival of Hurricane Belle on the eve of the show ensured that organizers would learn to swim in the deep end of the pool. The team, however, was up to the challenge.

"It was really very, very hairy," Tinka said, recalling the stables and tents that blew down, the horses that were evacuated. "It was scary, but it was exciting with the storm. It didn't even seem bleak. We had a job to do and we knew we would do it."

The inaugural organizers did do it, pulling off the show despite their relative inexperience and despite a hurricane. They also did it despite a fickle response from potential sponsors. Interest among sponsors, of course, has since run to the opposite extreme. But in the early days, the Classic had to scramble.

"That first year we had tables for sale in the Grand Prix tent," Tinka said. "We tried to sell them for a few hundred dollars. We had to have a cocktail party to get people interested in buying a table. Now we have a waiting list."

The same went for the Boutique Gardens. "That first year we had to beg people to come for practically nothing," Tinka recalled. "Now they beg us."

Topping served as chairwoman when the show debuted in 1977 as the Hampton Classic. As the show grew, she and others in-

Tinka Topping & daughter, Jenno at the 1979 Hampton Classic.

volved realized that more elaborate organization was needed. A Board of Directors was formed. Tinka was a charter member, and remains so into the mid-90's. She did, however, relinquish the chairwoman's post to Agneta Currey. In addition, executive directors were named: Anthony Hitchcock and Jean Lindgren, a couple that had catered the 1976 show. Under the hand of all these people, the Classic would grow into the prestigious event it is today.

Tinka continued to play a key role in the growing years. She served on the Board; she handled the awards portion of the show - the trophies, the ceremonies, the sponsors. Was it an easy job? Let's just say Tinka learned how to improvise.

"I used to grab someone out of the Grand Prix tent that looked famous and say, 'Come out and award this trophy'", Tinka said. "Now they're standing in line waiting to be asked to do it".

"Then one year it was so muddy I thought I was going to die. I was running back and forth with the mud up to here," Tinka added, pointing to her shins. "I was barefoot and bleeding and I had to get a tetanus shot. And I thought, what am I doing? I'm a grown up woman with four children."

One of those children, her daughter Jenno, was a big rider on the national circuit. Throughout the 80's, Jenno's riding, Tinka's organizational duties and Bud's work as head groundskeeper made the Classic a big affair for the Toppings. These were golden years.

The sparkle would fade. When a close friend, trainer Robert Hoskins, died in the early 1990's, the Classic lost some of its luster for Tinka. "I think I lost heart when he died," she says. "I didn't want to be as involved after that."

By then, the Classic didn't need her guiding hand as much as it had in the early years. The child, as it were, had grown. A mother could only look back and marvel.

"What happened? Why did it become so fashionable? God only knows," Tinka said. "I guess it was done right. Everything we tried to do, we tried to do beautifully."

Pinning of a ribbon at the 1966 Southampton Horse Show.   *Photo courtesy of Tinka Topping*

brought in. In 1985, a series of violent storms descended upon the show. Heavy rains fell. Tornadoes even touched down here and there across the South Fork. The twisters missed the show grounds, but the problem of stormwater remained. Some makeshift, emergency measures did the trick. By Grand Prix Sunday, the place was dried out. Fittingly the sun shone on what was at the time a record crowd.

The 1989 show saw another silver lining. Shortly before the show, two prominent riders, Michael Matz and his future wife D.D. Alexander, were aboard a United Air Lines DC-10 that crashed in Sioux City, Iowa. Both survived a tragedy that claimed the lives of 114 others. Amazingly, both made it to the Classic. More amazing, both won big. Alexander won a jumping event on Saturday. The next day, Matz won the Grand Prix and, in the process, the hearts of the Classic crowd.

As for the Classic, it has survived much that fate can possibly deal large events: Hurricanes, floods, a predecessor whose flame flickered, but never completely died. The show is about as battle-tested as it gets. Maybe that was why when Hurricane Bob visited a week before the show in 1991, it seemed nothing more than a passing shower. There was damage, there was destruction. But the show went on without a hitch.

The Hampton Classic has always gone on. It has become the prototypical horse show that all others strive to emulate. The 1995 Classic marks the show's 20th anniversary. But in actuality, Classic roots trace back nearly 100 years. Like any centenarian, it continues to amaze. Like any centenarian, it is a survivor.

Chapter II: Behind the Scenes

The Organization

Understand this about the Hampton Classic: It is not just any American outdoor horse show. It is THE American outdoor horse show. With its size, duration, popularity, attendance figures, sponsorship rolls and organization, the Classic is the show all the others want to be.

Who says? The people who show. They go to the Classic, they go to the others. They see the difference.

"There are some things that could be handled better at the Classic, but compared to the other shows it's at the top of the heap," said Alvin Topping of Bridgehampton's Swan Creek Farms. "Every year there are questionnaires handed out and there are very, very few complaints about how that show was run."

"We go to a lot of different shows, but they're not as nice as the Classic," said trainer Bobby Ginsberg. "The Hampton Classic really goes all out."

Perhaps the best assessment comes from someone familiar with shows all across the country. That would be Michael Parish, president of the National Grand Prix League. The Hampton Classic, he said, "is the epitome of show riding in the United States. It combines excellence in terms of preparation. The exhibitors, the owners and riders can all appreciate the effort that goes into producing an excellent show with lots of spec-

Show preparation starts at the home of executive directors Tony Hitchock and Jean Lindgren in Sagaponack before moving over to the show grounds on Snake Hollow Road, where Bob Drennan awaits with awards.

Jean Lindgren and Tony Hitchcock at the 1994 Patron's Party.

tators, lots of coverage in the media, lots of sponsorships, lots of prize money. All phases of the show would rank among the best in the United States."

Need an international perspective? Says Tim Grubb, the Grand Prix rider originally from England, "it's one of the nicest shows in the world, this."

The Classic has risen to the top of the national outdoor show scene in relatively short time. By the advent of the 1990's, a show that had debuted just 14 years before was being called the country's biggest. Given that the show was fairly small for its first few years, it could be said the Classic went big time in less than a decade.

How did it get there? A combination of factors. Ambitious, diligent people run the show. They've put in not only the requisite time, they've reinvested, making improvements, no matter how minor, a point of every show. This may seem simple, but not all horse shows do it. For the Classic, it's made a discernible difference.

The Classic has also benefited from location. In the Hamptons, the Classic sits in the middle of a summer resort community that is home to the affluent and the famous. This has connected the show to wealthy and well-known patrons and sponsors, many of whom are involved in show riding in one way or another. On top of that, the Classic has become an entrenched part of the Hamptons social scene. As the Hamptons grew in the boom times of the mid 1980's, so, too, did the Classic. Combined, all the money, all the prestigious names and famous faces have given the Classic a social and financial dimension other shows can only envy. There are other, less glitzy reasons. The Classic's true foundation is the surrounding community. The show is run by locals and has always tendered the services of local business. Obviously, it helps when you can call the Hamptons home. But on the bottom line, the Classic is intertwined with its host community. That's a bond and source of stability most other shows don't have.

Ultimately, a show can be no better than the people who run it. What is remarkable is that the Hampton Classic ascended under the leadership of people who had little previous experience running horse shows. Tinka Topping, the show's original chairwoman, did have experience, but only with smaller events like the old Southampton Horse

Agneta Currey puts her touch on the Grand Prix ring.

Show. Topping's successor, Agneta Currey, was a complete newcomer. And Tony Hitchcock and Jean Lindgren, the executive directors? Their first taste of the Classic came through a catering job.

"No one had any great experience in running a horse show," Currey recalled. "We all had to learn from our mistakes. We borrowed from others. That's what I did. I borrowed like crazy."

As a native of Sweden, Currey drew from European shows. One element in particular was decor. Great emphasis was placed on landscaping, gardening, and jump decoration. Currey wanted a show that looked good. And, indeed, the good looks came through accretion. Each year, little by little, the grounds were en-

hanced. The footing was improved; many plants and trees brought in for a show were kept and made permanent.

The Classic, with the voluntary help of an army of local nurseries, built up its own little show world behind the McNamara farmhouse on Snake Hollow Road. Picturesque grounds have been the result.

Currey says the techniques used in landscaping were a model followed by the whole show. In all aspects, she said, Classic organizers strove to make improvements every year. They also strove to get local people involved. The combination of the two, Currey speculates, has been the key to the Classic's success.

"We did it very slowly, a little every year," the chairwoman

said. "If you can improve one thing each year, I think that's the accomplishment. Some people make a living off a horse show and don't put anything back into the show. That's why most shows don't improve. We put in a lot every year. We try to improve the show one way or another. That's the only reason we got better than the other shows."

As a show staged in a well-to-do corner of the world, the Classic perhaps could afford to re-invest more so than other shows. Still, the Classic is a source of livelihood for some, and it is a benefit for the local hospital. Like any enterprise, it needs to make money and pay its bills - bills that steadily grew with the show. By the mid-90's, the Classic was costing $1.6 million to put on.

Profile: Agneta Currey

There are many reasons why the Hampton Classic has become the nation's top outdoor show. Here's one: Agneta Currey.

Currey has been chairwoman of the Hampton Classic since the early 1980's, when original chair Tinka Topping asked her to take over. As someone who showed horses at the Classic, Currey felt obligated to accept. But she does suspect that a penchant for complaining - she found the footing particularly poor - may have forced her to put effort where her mouth was.

"I thought it was my duty, my turn, because I was involved with the show and I felt I should pay my dues," Currey recalls. "I don't know why I was asked. I had no experience and I'm not well organized. Maybe I complained too much."

Powerful, but personable and unassuming, Currey is a big Hampton Classic wheel in a small package. Make that small and spunky. She is petite, but don't call her dainty. A practice spill (Currey does ride) just before the 1994 show knocked out three front teeth. Currey bounced back, saw the dentist and was on hand for Opening Day.

Currey must be tough. After all, it has been under her watch that the Classic has evolved into the nation's biggest outdoor horse show, which makes it seem strange she had absolutely no organizational experience when she came on board.

It must have been the European touch. Currey was born and raised in Sweden. In 1961, she came stateside and met future husband Brownlee Currey, a newspaper publisher from Nashville. The Curreys maintain a home in Tennessee, as well as a summer home in Southampton.

It was in the Hamptons that Currey got involved with horses. She started riding with her kids, who trained at Topping Riding Club in Sagaponack. (Her son Christian has emerged as a top junior jumper.) While hanging around and watching, Currey figured she might as well ride, too. She will tell you quite plainly, though, that despite diligent training, even at the hand of Olympians Joe Fargis and Conrad Homfeld, she hasn't gotten much better.

"I haven't progressed much," Currey admits. "I've taken thousands of lessons; I've had endless trainers. I'm a slow learner, you could say."

Fortunately for the Classic, Currey was a fast study in horse show organization. She came to the chair with no experience, yet helped turn the Classic into the best. Like her fellow organizers, Currey learned from trial and error. She also borrowed liberally from other shows she had seen, particularly in Europe. But her real secret, the one that emerges when you watch her at work on the show? Just plain hustle and dedication. "Chairwoman" is not just some title for Currey. It is a role.

Her pet project has always been grounds improvement. With the help of fellow Board member Daphne Marinovich and Southampton florist Maureen Matthews, Currey went in heavy for landscaping. Each year more trees and shrubs and hedges and other plantings were made permanent pieces of the Classic grounds. Currey got local florists and nurseries involved, bartering exposure for work. By the mid-90's, two dozen local businesses were involved in sprucing up grounds regarded to be the best in the American show jumping world.

Currey will tell you it is exactly that combination of annual improvement and community involvement that has been the key to the Classic's success. That's true. But others say it's been the work of organizers like Currey that has made the ultimate difference.

"I tell you what, if it wasn't for her wanting it to be the best, it would have been hard to get it where it is today," said show manager Steve Stephens. "She'd seen enough other shows to know how to make it better. She loves it. She's been at it a long time. I like working for someone like that. It gives you the "wants.""

Nowadays, Currey questions her desire. Maybe, she says, it's time to hand the reins to someone else. But then the show comes, and Currey is right back at it.

Stick around the grounds any night of show week. The riding is long over for the day, the crowds have gone home, the Grand Prix Tent entertaining is through, the sun is sinking. The ring is left to work crews who rearrange the Grand Prix course. One small, slight woman in a wide-brimmed hat moves among them in the gathering dusk, meticulously decorating the jumps with fresh-cut flowers. Stick around. Now you know why the show is so good.

Agneta Currey with Grand Prix course designer Conrad Homfeld.

So Classic organizers had to be good business people. They needed sponsors and advertisers. In the early days, the sponsors weren't lining up as they are today. The Classic had to go after them. Some came readily. Show riding is a money sport, and a few big corporations already had ties to the game. The top guns of several of the Classic's more well-known sponsors - Calvin Klein, Hearst Magazines, Nine West - all have family members who ride. Their sponsorship was more or less a natural.

Others were lured in. With the use of promotional tapes, the Classic solicited new sponsors. The sight of top-flight riding, cheering crowds and the ruffling banners of other corporations was enticing. Some big names were already involved. Thus, the show took on the aura of a "must" promotion. From there, it snowballed. The effect was much the same when it came to soliciting patrons for the Grand Prix tent. Once a few key names were aboard, the others fell into place.

Classic promotion thrives because the show is always wheeling out new ideas. In the summer of 1994, show organizers unveiled a promo package called "August is Hampton Classic Month." Geared toward East End merchants, it was basically a co-op advertising strategy. In exchange for using the Classic's name in their ads (i.e. "August is Hampton Classic Month at Mom & Pop's"), merchants were asked to launch ad campaigns that included promos for the Classic. There were other facets to the

Above: Show Manager Steve Stephens. Below: Classic President Dennis Suskind.

Banners of some of the Hampton Classic's biggest sponsors, including Crown Royal, Calvin Klein and Harper's Bazaar fly high over the Grand Prix grandstands. Sponsors do not lack for exposure.

deal. In exchange for a week of passes, merchants took out full-page ads in the show program and agreed to donate a pre-determined sales percentage to charity.

The whole business of sponsorship occupies its own little universe of the show, one to which the Classic gives top priority. As with the locals, the Classic works a cooperative angle with its bigger sponsors. In particular, the Classic is a big endorser of cross-sponsorships, strategies in which various patrons team up on a project. This helps spread out the cost and labor and also makes the idea of sponsorship a bit more palatable.

An example: the World of the Horse exhibition on Opening Day is presented by Nine West, the women's shoe manufacturer, and organized by the Nassau-Suffolk Horseman's Association. Crown Royal and Harper's Bazaar team up for the $100,000 Grand Prix. Kid's Day, a new event that debuted in 1994, was underwritten by Newsday, Donna Karan and Barnes & Noble Bookstores.

What needs sponsorship at the Classic? Just about everything. By 1994, the show was costing $1.6 million to stage. While the Classic does use the old-fashioned barter system as much as it can, such as with the

landscapers and volunteer workers from Southampton Hospital, the show carries large expenses. All those temporary tents, stables and grandstands are a big outlay. In 1994, the stabling tents alone cost more than $100,000, according to show manager, Steve Stephens. There are additional expenses: the full-time staff, the hired staff for show week, prizes, the property lease, the scoreboard rental, the program printing. "It's an expensive ordeal to put this show on," said Press Officer Diana De Rosa.

The Classic revenues? Posters, shirts and other memorabilia and ticket sales. Food concessionaires pay a flat fee and

The 1994 Patron's Party at Stephanie Powers's Five Tails Farm. David Feldman of Today's Man was the party sponsor.

also turn in a percentage of their revenues during the week. Exhibitors in the Boutique Gardens pay $1,200 to set up shop. Riders must pay to show.

The key dollars come from the sponsors and the table patrons. The average corporate sponsor shells out between $10,000 and $25,000. Many sponsorships run higher. The dollar signs affixed to the bigger events are a testament to that: the $100,000 Crown Royal Grand Prix, the $25,000 Calvin Klein Show Jumping Derby and $10,000 CK Equitation Classic, the $25,000 Sally Hansen Grand Prix and the $15,000 Town and Country Junior Amateur Owner Jumper Classic.

Those are some of the more visible sponsorships. Others are a bit more behind the scenes. The Sponsor and Patron party, held a few weeks before show time, was paid for by Today's Man in 1994. The $5,000 Hunter Classic? The sponsorship fee was picked up by Barnes & Noble. Sponsorship of the press tent was carried by Jerry & David's Red House Market.

"No other show that I know of in the United States, no other show attracts the corporate sponsorship the Hampton Classic does," said Diana De Rosa. "Still, even with all that money, it's hard to have money left over at the end."

The Classic's average gross receipts are approximately $1.75 million. Whatever is left over after the bills are paid is donated to Southampton Hospital, the U.S. Equestrian Team and the Juvenile Diabetes Foundation. The hospital alone has received approximately half a million over the course of the show's history.

Who are the people responsible for bringing the Classic to the top? When the show first started making its climb, the organizers, while relatively inexperienced, weren't exactly on their own. They enjoyed the services of pro show manager Steve Stephens of Palmetto, Florida. Stephens, the owner of a jump design and manufacturing company, would arrive shortly before the show. He'd bring in his jumps and handle all the riding logistics, which entailed matching ring capacity and class size to set up show schedules. He was, at the time, the pro among the amateurs. ("We never would have gotten out of the mud and dust without Steve Stephens," said Agneta Currey.) Stephens, who is still with the show, though now as a pro among other pros, deflects the credit. The Classic has emerged, he says, because of the efforts of its year-round caretakers. "You couldn't put one of these shows on every other week," he said. "You couldn't put on four of these shows in a year. You need 11 months of preparation and getting ready - mentally, physically, in all ways."

Indeed, as the Classic has grown, so has the requisite prep time. Running a week-long show of this magnitude is a year-round task. There is some down time. In the winter, Hitchcock and Lindgren trek out to California to run the Desert Circuit, in itself a model show. Back at home, Dawn Dunn, the general assistant, works year-round on the show. As the show approaches, Sag Harbor bookkeeper Troy Powell keeps busy with the ledgers. Abbie Hitchcock, Tony's daughter, handles secretarial chores. David Dimijian handles the sign work. Diana De Rosa, the press officer, was hired in the early 90's. With the advent of TV coverage in the late 1980's, David Hoffman was brought on as television coordinator. Outside, head groundskeeper Bud Topping tends to the greens and to site improvements throughout the year.

So the wheel is always in spin. It just spins slower in the winter. By May, the pace starts picking up. That's when the staff begins meeting with sponsors and advertisers. Requests for a shop in the Boutique Gardens, for a table under the Grand Prix tent are fielded. Press credentials are attended to, the annual program is written and printed. A show budget is drawn up, a prize list and exhibitors index amassed. It all starts in May and gets busier and busier as summer marches inexorably to show week.

Up until the week before the show, all the prep work is done at the Hitchcock home in Sagaponack. The whole place seems given over to the production. Four different computer systems are on-line. The home atmosphere helps to ease the stress. But, as Jean will tell you if you inquire about the timing of a visit, "there is no good time."

Busy on the Home Front. Above: Executive Director Anthony Hitchcock works on one of the four Classic computer systems set up in his house. Left: Hitchcock's daughter Abbie works the phones.

Still, it beats an office. Most of the staff, Tony and Jean included, roam around barefoot and in shorts. Each day, the crew breaks for lunch religiously at 12:30. (Please don't call for a half hour.)

Hitchcock is at the head of this entourage. He is described by those who work with him as a take-charge "ideas" guy who is aptly surrounded by efficient follow-through people. He is, they say, uncowed by challenge. No task, no problem ever seems to be too steep. The work ethic is reportedly infectious. The staff follows his lead. So, apparently, do all those other shows.

"It takes a tremendous staff and 12 months out of the year to put that show on," said Michael Parish, the Grand Prix League president. "I think what Tony has done is raise the standard. The standard other shows aspire to is a lot higher now. The Classic is a role model for a lot of shows."

"This show is the number one premier show in the United States," said Steve Stephens, who manages other shows during the course of the year. "I would say that even if I wasn't the show manager. I think it compares ... there is no comparison."

Classic staffers handling the behind-the-scenes work include (from top) Dawn Dunn, Diana De Rosa, Troy Powell (with Jean Lindgren) and Adam Silfen.

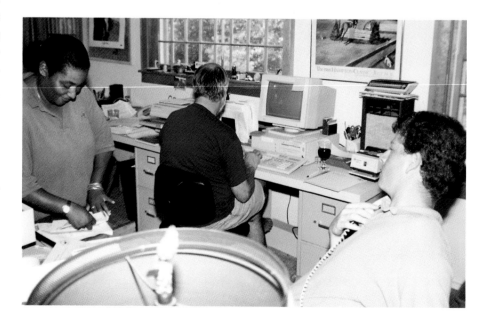

Sitting on the Board

The Hampton Classic Board of Directors reflects the crosscut of the different, but interrelated streams that flow into the Classic pool. There are local people, there are those who swim in broader waters. There are horse riders, there are horse owners, there are business people. Together, they oversee the show and, according to the woman who sits at the head of it all, Chairwoman Agneta Currey, manage to get along quite well.

"We want to mix it all up so we cover the bases," Currey said. "It's a friendly group of people. It's not like anybody orders anyone to do something."

If cooperation is a key, so is clout. Through the array of people on its Board - there are 25 in all - the Classic has, to its great advantage, been able to make inroads into various segments of both the corporate and equestrian world.

"The Board members of the Hampton Classic, with the exception of me, are members of other Boards with incredible access," said charter member Kelsey Marechal of Sagaponack. "We have some very heavy hitters who are directors of this show."

The president of the Classic is Dennis Suskind, who has lent considerable business expertise to the show. He is retired partner of Goldman Sachs, having spent much of his early career in the firm's J. Aaron precious metals division. He now lives in Bridgehampton.

Of the other locals, Kelsey Marechal and Tinka Topping are all that remain of the original Board that resurrected the Southampton Horse Show back in the early 1970's. They are part of the local connection that includes Anne and Emily Aspinall, the sisters who run Topping Riding Club.

Elaine Benson, the proprietor of the eponymous gallery in Bridgehampton, came on originally through her role as publicity director for Southampton Hospital. She now heads the committee that selects the annual show poster.

All Board members take on committee assignments. Merely getting on the Board isn't the end-all of being a member. You've got to earn your keep, says Marechal. Emily Aspinall, for instance, has the task of handling prizes, which entails trophies, sponsors, presentations. She is aided by Ross Runnels Jr., a longstanding member who works as an industrial design consultant. The Boutique Gardens are overseen by Diane Brennan. The former proprietor of Brennan's Bit & Bridle Shop in Bridgehampton, Brennan is an original member of the Classic Board. Many riders dot the Board. Conrad

Classic Board members (clockwise from top left) Kelsey Marechal, Helen Stevens, Alessandro di Montezemolo and Ross Runnels Jr.

Homfeld and Joe Fargis came to the table following their Olympic feats of 1984, adding international prestige to what was then still a relatively local show. Sale Johnson, Kelly Klein and Patricia Raynes are other well-known riders on the Board. All are relatively new members. All are sponsors. Kelly Klein, of course, is the wife of Calvin Klein, one of the Classic's top patrons.

Lisa Tarnopol, a recent addition, is the daughter of former Classic president Michael Tarnopol. An international rider, Tarnopol does have a local connection as the former proprietor of a Bridgehampton horse farm. William Mann, one of the Classic's earliest sponsors and Grand Prix patrons, also has a local farm connection. His wife Lydia Mann used to own Southampton's Sandron Farm.

Another long-running sponsor who sits on the Board is Helen Stevens. She and her husband Whitney have long sponsored the Grand Prix qualifying class, which bears their name.

Business connections are varied. Earle Macke came in as a sports promoter and as a horseman involved with racehorses. He was part owner of Mill Pearl, the horse Fargis rode to Olympic gold. The world of fashion is represented through Catherine and Alessandro Di Montezemolo. Catherine, a former editor, used to stage the Classic fashion show with Board member Ann Lawrence. Charles Dolan is the chairman of Cablevision. He is also the father of Grand Prix rider Debbie Dolan. Linda Robinson, a recent addition, runs a Manhattan public relations business. She came to the Classic through showing horses and helping out. Daphne Marinovich, another new member, also came aboard via working the show. Lyn Silfen is a long-time Classic sponsor with her husband.

Raising the Show

For much of the year, the 60 acres that are home to the Hampton Classic lie empty. Just open fields gently sloping from an old country road down to Long Pond, fields divided only by the hedges and trees and shrubs the Classic has planted over the years.

The property is owned by the McNamara family, whose home sits shrouded in trees at the head of the grounds. The Classic leases the land and maintains it. The guy who rides point on that train is Bud Topping. He is the head groundskeeper. Throughout the year, Bud tends to the Classic turf. He'll drive over from his Sagaponack farm in one of his pickup trucks with the family dog "Bigfoot" riding shotgun. He keeps the grass watered and cut. He tends to site improvements, whether they be related to sprinklers, storm drains or electrical systems.

Bud is an old hand at this. Back in Sagaponack, he and his wife Tinka Topping used to host the Southampton Horse Show. But the Hampton Classic works on a bigger scale, one that turns 60 empty acres into a veritable city of tents and stables and trailers and show rings.

While keeping up the grounds is a year-round chore, the major work doesn't really kick in until mid-July. That's when the site starts being prepared for show time in earnest. The dramatic changes, though, aren't really seen until about ten days before the show. That's when all the tents go up. It comes

The Bridgehampton grounds that host the Hampton Classic are nothing but empty fields for most of the year. Keeping the grounds in shape and getting them ready for the show is the job of head groundskeeper Bud Topping, who is pictured above. Opposite: Grounds coordinator Neil O'Connor gives the crew an order; Dave Reade responds.

fast, seemingly overnight. Brandywine of Maryland comes in and puts up the stabling tents - a dozen 60x300 canvasses in all. At the same time, Party Time of Poughkeepsie sets up the Grand Prix and boutique tents. For two solid days the grounds ring with the sound of sledgehammers driving stakes. There is pounding, then quiet, as the tents, laid out flat, are raised and tied down by rope. One goes up about every hour until the Classic skyline is complete. Over on the other side of the Grand Prix ring Chair Hire of New Jersey builds up the grandstand. The gray steel-bar skeleton goes up, then the green planks are overlaid.

Topping oversees the whole production along with grounds coordinator Neil O'Connor. All the tents and bleachers are up by the time Steve Stephens and his trucks roll in several days before the show. Stephens, the show manager, owns a jump manufacturing business. Most of the jumps you

This page: Spikes, hammers, knots and lines are the tools of the tent trade. At the Classic, two firms need just two days to erect the show's canvas skyline. All tents go up less than a week before show time. Opposite page: The grandstands reach the sky. At ground level, the jump crew starts unloading the rails and the standards show manager Steve Stephens has brought up from Florida.

see at the Classic - the rails, the standards - are his. They are trucked in, crammed end to end in two tractor trailers. There are that many. They have to fill six competition rings and five practice rings.

While the jumps are being unloaded, washed and erected, landscapers are busy in the show rings, planting new trees and flowers, tidying up permanent displays. Miki Gilsenan, who has been with the Classic since 1985, oversees this department. So does Maureen Matthews of Southampton's Flowers Inc. She co-chairs the Classic's grounds committee with Agneta Currey and Daphne Marinovich. As we've seen, landscaping is a big source of pride for the Classic. The grounds have been steadily built up. Each year new plantings come in. The Classic holds on to what it can and provides a permanent home. Thus have jump decorations sprouted in the Grand Prix ring. Thus have ring hedges grown more encompassing each season. In 1994, 104 tubs of arborvitae were added to the hunter and jumper rings. As show time nears, Matthews and Gilsenan and all the other green thumbs are out in the sun, digging, trimmimg and planting. Local nurseries are there too. Most tend to the same plantings every year. Frankenbach's Garden Center of Southampton landscapes the Grand Prix tent entrances. Fred Petta of Warren's Garden Center in Water Mill spruces up his handiwork around the Grand Prix bank.

The new comes in as well. Dorothy Carter - Clarke of Carter's Landscaping in East Quogue puts the finishing touches on a water garden she built in memory of her brother, George Carter. Over in the Grand Prix ring, flat upon flat of dahlias go in along the inside wall. A floral rainbow edges the green expanse.

"This was once a potato field," Matthews says. "Never forget that."

"This is a major production," Gilsenan notes. "This is the Hamptons, after all."

By the end of the week most everything is up: the tents, the stands, the stables, the flowers. The sun goes down on a Friday night in the last of summer. Swallows dart and dive over the green fields, the blue and yellow-striped tents, the empty green bleachers. The place is empty, yet so full of anticipation. Patron banners ruffle in the breeze high over the Grand Prix ring. Concessionaires quietly bring in their wares. Sprinklers whisk in the dying light. Bud Topping, still in his faded white t-shirt, tinkers on as dusk gathers. Don't you go home, Bud?

"This is home," he says with a wave

A cool wind blows; a red sun goes down. If the scene could be frozen here, before everything starts, before all the horses come, before all the people, too, it would still be the perfect show. Maybe better. But it can't be. Across the way, a passenger train pulls into the Bridgehampton station. A shrill whistle blows. The show, too, has arrived.

The George Carter Memorial Water Garden, built in 1994 by George's sister Dorothy Carter-Clarke. That's Classic landscaper Miki Gilsenan at the wheel.

ie Final Touches. Maureen Matthews decorates a waterwheel in the Grand Prix ring with hydrangeas. That's Classic Chairwoman
gneta Currey in the background.

Sunset at the Hampton Classic as seen from the Grand Prix ring. Overleaf: *An aerial view of the show just before Opening Day.*

(Aerial Photo by David Lynch/Eastern Aerial Photography.)

Chapter III: Show Time

The Hampton Classic comes in many facets. And while the social sheen that is so unique to the Classic often seems to outglitter all the rest, what lies at the heart of the show is the riding. It is the lone necessity, of course. Take away the riding and there is no show, no big-money sponsors, no Grand Prix tent, no big-name stars.

At the Hampton Classic, well over 1,000 riders and well over 1,000 horses show each year. Among that number are some of the top names in the show jumping world. They come because the Classic is such a big, can't-miss show.

Riding is omnipresent at the Classic. With the exception of one day, it goes down from morning to night for a week, with dozens of classes showing in five different rings. To the uninitiated, all that riding in all those rings can seem a kaleidoscopic blur. And the unending stream of class names coming over the loudspeaker - the Green Hunter, the Maiden Equitation, the Amateur-Owner Jumper - can heighten the confusion. Many a newcomer has no doubt been left wondering, "just what exactly is it I'm watching anyway?"

For starters, a broad perspective is in order. The riding seen at the Hampton Classic is what is known as the English tradition. English riding puts great emphasis on appearance, manners and style. It is deliberately showy, elegant and formal, as compared to the rougher utilitarian style of Western riding. The image of Western riding is the cowboy out on the trail. The image of English riding is the aristocrat out on the fox hunt. Western riding has its rodeos; English riding has its horse shows.

You should also know this about show riding: It is an acme of sexual equality in sport. There are no separate divisions for male and female riders, or horses. Everything is on equal footing. There are no handicaps, no ladies tees. All compete in the same ring with equal chance for victory.

When it comes to show time, events like the Hampton Classic feature two basic types of competition: jumping and hunting. The jumping is just

what it implies. Horses and riders are out to cleanly jump all obstacles and do it within a given amount of time. It is an objective event. Form, appearance mean nothing. There is no judging. The clock, the fault count keep the score. On the other hand, form and appearance mean everything in the Hunter Division. This is a judged event, and judges are looking at everything from the braids on the horse to its stride and jumping style. There is a major division known as Equitation. In Equitation, it is the rider who is judged, not the horse.

Before getting a detailed look at these divisions and the various classes they encompass, you should know that the Hampton Classic is not an entity unto itself when it comes to show riding. It is part of a cycle that plays out every year - a cycle that, here in the East, runs from Florida in the early winter months, through the Northeast in the spring and summer, to ultimately the major indoor shows in the fall.

In a way, show riding is much like baseball, basketball and other sports more familiar to the average sports fan. Standings are kept. They are based on "game" results, except in this case the games are individual shows, like the Hampton Classic, that are member events of a particular circuit. In a sense, the shows comprise the "regular season." Like baseball teams, riders hope to accumulate enough wins, or points, to qualify for the playoffs, which in the American horse world are the big indoor shows in late autumn. Basically, the Washington International Horse Show and National Horse Show comprise the World Series of show riding.

How big a role does the Classic play in all this? Well, because of its timing in late summer, its A-3 rating, its size and its big cash purses, the Classic stands out in the chase for the post-season like a pennant drive in baseball. It can factor heavily into who goes to the finals and who stays home.

Geographically, the equestrian world in the United States is divided into three regions: East, Midwest and West. All operate under the jurisdiction of the American Horse Show Associa-

tion, the governing body of show riding in the country. Each of the three regions keeps separate standings during the regular season. Riders are based in one, but are not prevented from competing in others. At the end of the year, the top riders and horses from each region go on to compete in the national finals.

Each region has a series of leagues to accommodate the varying skill levels of horse and rider. At the top of the heap are the National Grand Prix League and the American Grandprix Association. This is the league that features the Grand Prix jumpers, the people who compete in the $100,000 Crown Royal Grand Prix at the Hampton Classic. The National Grand Prix League, of which the Hampton Classic is a member, has divisions in the East, Midwest and West regions. It is, in keeping with our baseball analogy, the major leagues of show jumping, as is the A.G.A.

There are several "minor" leagues. As in baseball, these leagues do not feature the caliber of ability found in the majors, but are often proving grounds for the stars of tomorrow. In show riding, the minors include the Miller's League, presented by Marshall and Sterling, for children and amateur adult jumpers. The Ritz-Carlton League features competition in the same classes. Both leagues are for riders who want to compete in a Grand Prix setting, but do not yet have the ability to compete at the Grand Prix level.

As riders improve they advance to the NGL/Sprint Junior/Amateur-Owner Series. This league features show jumping on a higher level than Miller's

and Ritz-Carlton. It is essentially the Triple A of show riding. The next step up is the Grand Prix League.

In Hunter competition, the American Hunter-Jumper Foundation gives out national awards each year to the top pony, junior, amateur-owner and professional riders. The foundation gives out annual awards on a regional level in the same classes, as well as in adult amateur and children's divisions. As in jump-

ing, Miller's offer leagues for children and amateur adult hunters, leagues in which riders compete for points that qualify them for national finals.

Then there is Equitation. This division has about a half dozen national competitions in which running point standings are kept and year-end finals are held. AHSA Medal and ASPCA Maclay are two of the entry-level national competitions. Further up the ladder come national eq-

uitation series, all separate from one another, sponsored by the Washington International Horse Show, the Professional Horsemen's Association (PHA) and the U.S. Equestrian Team.

Now, not every show is a member event of every league. How does the Classic fit in? Prominently. For one, the Classic's $25,000 Calvin Klein Show Jumping Derby is one of the bigger and richer events on the 29-show tour of the NGL/Sprint Junior/Amateur-Owner Series. The Classic is also a member of the Miller's children & amateur adult leagues in both hunters and jumpers. The Classic also hosts a qualifying class for the Washington International Equitation Classic. It is a member event of Medal, Maclay, PHA and USET equitation. On top of all that comes the Crown Royal Grand Prix. The Classic's

Riding at the Classic runs a range of emotion, from anxious waiting to glory to disappointment to camaraderie. Among the riders pictured in this collage is Kelly Klein. She's wearing the derby at left.

headlining event is a big stop for the National Grand Prix League. Its $100,000 payoff is one of the nation's richest. The big payoff, the show's prestige, make the Classic a major Grand Prix League stop no rider wants to miss.

"The Hampton Classic is a show we've always done," said Mark Leone, the youngest of three brothers who rides in the Grand Prix League's Eastern Conference. "It's always been a biggie for us and for everybody on the East Coast. It's got money, it's got atmosphere, it's got spectators. On the competitive level, you've got the best riders going for money in a beautiful ring on good horses over a tough course. This is an important stop on the tour. It's always important to make a good showing here."

"Basically, the cream of the crop will come here," said Michael Endicott, a Grand Prix

rider from California. "They say if you do well here, you can do well anywhere."

"As far as being an event with quality horses and riders, as well as being an event that has captured the imagination of the show jumping world, the Hampton Classic is in a world of its own," said Michael Parish, president of the National Grand Prix League. "Everyone likes to show there."

"Because of the prize money, because of the setting in the Hamptons, because of the top course designers and top grounds, these are all reasons why we bring in the top riders in the country," asserted Diana De Rosa, the Classic's Press Officer.

The dollar signs cannot be downplayed. While it may be true money can't buy everything, in the National Grand Prix League it buys points. It's a

simple equation. The more prize money riders win, the more points they accrue in the standings. And so the top riders come - and not only the Grand Prix types. Big points are up for grabs on all levels. With its A-3 rating, the Classic has the maximum number of available points at an individual show. Example: a sixth-place ribbon from an A-3 show like the Classic is worth more points than a first-place ribbon at an A-1 show.

"You say your horse won at the Hampton Classic Grand Prix, or any ribbon here, that really means something," said John Lytle, a trainer who works at Southampton's Clearview Farm in the summer and in Florida in the winter. "It's so competitive. A lot of people work all summer long with the Classic in mind."

By the time they hit the Classic, riders are already deep into the season. In the East, the

Left: *Grand Prix star Michael Endicott.* Above: *A rider measures up the competition.* Opposite Page: *Terry Regan and Manassas County take a blue.*

yearly cycle opens in January and February with the 10-week winter series in Florida. As winter gives way to March and April, the tour moves steadily northward, via Virginia and Pennsylvania. In early May, the Garden State Horse Show hosts a key Grand Prix League event in Augusta, N.J. More big shows follow on the heels of that. North Salem, N.Y., hosts two Grand Prix League events with the Children's Services Horse Show and the Old Salem Farm Show. The Devon Horse Show in Pennsylvania, held over Memorial Day Weekend is another big date. Devon drips with prestige. It is one of the oldest shows in the country.

The tour stays up north during the summer months, with key shows such as Lake Placid, the Ox Ridge Charity show in Darien, Ct. and the Hartwood Showjumping Festival in Pittsburgh. It is worth noting that most of these shows mentioned are big stops on the Eastern Conference national tour. There are other shows that are regionally oriented. On Long Island, for instance, A-rated shows can be found virtually every week of the summer.

National and local elements come together at the Hampton Classic, a show with a "Local Day" and a major Grand Prix League event serving as bookends. It is a very distinct show on the circuit. It is big, drawing some 1,400 entrants. It is long, sprawling over two weekends. It also has the distinction of drawing big crowds.

"The Classic stands out," says Swan Creek Farms owner

Alvin Topping, who regularly takes the riders he trains at his Bridgehampton farm to shows throughout the summer. "It's unique. Number one, the Classic is a major social event. The other shows have it, but it's not like this. The other thing is, the Clas-

sic has the room. They have the grounds. The facility they have is pretty much beyond the others' capacity just in size."

Where to after such a big show as the Classic? For the Grand Prix riders, the road leads south to Maryland and Delaware for the American Cafe Columbia Classic and the University of Delaware Jumper Classic. The grand prix at both are league events. For other riders, there are shows in New York, Vermont and Pennsylvania .

In all leagues, at all levels, it boils down to the big indoor trip. The points are tallied one last time and the top finishers move on to the finals at the National Horse Show and the Washington International. Fittingly, they are held in October - just like another Fall Classic.

Jumpers

Now that you know where the riding's come from and where it's going, you can better sort out the detailed divisions seen at the Classic. The place to start is with the jumpers, because jumpers comprise the class easiest for spectators to understand. The jumpers are also the most exciting.

It's pretty straightforward. Jumpers must jump the obstacles and do it within the allowed period of time. There is no judging involved, no weight placed on style or looks. Jumping events are a basic, but eye-opening test of speed and strength and nerve.

Varying levels of jumper classes are on display at the Classic. Some are based on the experience and prize winnings of the horses. Others are dictated by the age and experience of the riders. The range runs from children to amateurs to pros. The cream of the crop rises in the Open Jumper field. It is the class in which the top pros ride the top horses. This is the class that battles it out in the Grand Prix.

No matter what the level, all jumpers strive for the same thing as they navigate courses that typically feature 14-16 obstacles: A clean round. That means accruing no "faults," which are penalty points mistakes. Knockdowns, refusals are big no-nos. So are falls. So, too, is failure to finish on time.

The toll for mistakes is

Debbie Stephens with a "Blind Date" at the in-gate?

paid in faults. The fine depends on the offense. A knockdown - knocking down part of a jump - results in four faults. So does failure to clear a water jump. Refusals, which occur when a horse pulls up and "refuses" to jump an obstacle, amass in three-fault increments: three for the first, six for the second. Three strikes and you're out, as a third refusal results in elimination. There are other ways for horse and rider to get themselves eliminated. Falls, jumping the course out of order and failure to start at the proper time all spell automatic elimination.

The clock, of course, is a big factor in jumping competition. In all classes, riders must complete their round within a specified amount of time. For

each second over, one-quarter of a fault is assessed. Time is everything in the "speed" classes. These events are one round only, with the winner being decided by the fastest time and the fewest faults.

Most spectators are more familiar with "jump off" events such as the Grand Prix. These classes comprise two rounds. Riders who complete the first round fault-free qualify for the second round, which is the jump-off.

It is in the jump-off that jumping excitement reaches its peak. The course is shortened and made tougher. The time limit is tightened. Thus, the

This page: *Anne Kursinski, Michael Matz and Elizabeth Solter.* Bottom right: *Peter Leone of Team Leone.*

jump-off features the fastest riding over the toughest courses. The winner is typically the rider who finishes clean and with the fastest time. The fault system is still at play, with one exception: Time faults are now a full point.

Jumping competition, specifically the Grand Prix, offers the finest viewing at a horse show. At the Classic, jumper events are held in the Grand Prix and Jumper rings throughout the week, with the exception of Local Day. All sections, from children to pros, open their week with class competition. Class competition leads up to the bigger purse events at the end of the week. All events combine to determine the overall champions in each division at that particular show. That is why you will often see, say, the Leading Open Jumper of the week be someone other than the Grand Prix champ.

Here's the class breakdown of jumpers who ride the Classic, running from small to big.

*Children: This section features riders under the age of 18 who are competing strictly as children, as compared to the junior jumpers, who are also under 18 but can compete in other sections. Juniors also jump higher obstacles. Jumps in the Children's Division are no higher than 3'6".

Children jumpers compete in three classes to determine their champ. Any rider receiving a ribbon in any of the

three classes is eligible to compete in the $2,500 Children's Jumper Classic at the end of the week. It's a one-round deal. Fewest faults wins. A jump-off is used only to break a first-place tie. The event is a member of the Miller's Children's Jumper League.

*Adult Amateurs: This section features riders 18 and older competing strictly as amateurs. The section is lower on the ladder than the Amateur-Owner Division. Jumps are a 3'6" maximum.

Like the Children's Division, adult amateurs compete in three classes to determine an overall champion. Ribbons winners get a crack at the $2,500 Adult Jumper Classic to close out the week. The event is a

member of the Miller's Adult Jumper League.

*Juniors/Amateur-Owners: These two sections, while separate, share a lot of common ground, especially when it comes to the bigger purse events. The two sections mirror the children and adult amateurs as far as age goes. Juniors are under 18, amateur-owners 18 and over. There the similarity ends, because juniors and amateur-owners compete on a higher level. Their jumps range from 3'6" to 4'6". They can also compete in other divisions. Juniors and amateur-owners are second only to the Open Division pros.

Juniors and amateur-owners open their week separately with two $5,000 classes

each. Amateur-owners, it must be noted, are subdivided into "high" and "low" classes, the distinction being the height of the jumps. Later in the week, juniors and amateur-owners come together in the bigger events, the hot tamale being the $25,000 Calvin Klein Show Jumping Derby. This is one of the Classic's centerpiece jumping events, second only to the Grand Prix. It is a showcase for future stars. Appropriately, it is held on Grand Prix Sunday. Riders first have to qualify for the Calvin Klein Derby. They do so in the Hampton Classic Derby Welcome Stake on Friday. Those who don't make the cut have the consolation of the $25,000 Sally Hansen Grand Prix or the $15,000 Town & Country Jumper Classic on Saturday. The top riders go to

Sunday's Calvin Klein derby, which is one of the bigger events in the NGL/Sprint Junior/Amateur-Owner Jumper Series. The Calvin Klein Show Jumping Derby, along with the other events in this class, also helps determine the overall junior and amateur-owner champs at the Classic.

*Preliminary Jumpers: This section is determined not by the experience of the rider, but of the horse. Preliminaries are horses that have won less than $2,500 as a jumper. Horses who have eclipsed the $2,500 mark can still compete in this section if they are in their first year of showing. The Preliminary Section at the Hampton Classic is divided by jump height, with the high classes ranging from 3'9" to 4'6" and the low classes from 3'6" to 4'3".

*Open Jumpers: Here is where you find the big boys (and the big girls). Here is also where you find the top horses, the big prize winners. Open jumping is the peak of competition at all A-rated horse shows. The jumps stand as high as five feet three inches. The spreads are often more than five feet across.

At the Classic, the Open Jumpers start with several classes before drawing a bead on the $25,000 Stevens Grand Prix Qualifier on Friday. This event determines who will go to the $100,000 Crown Royal Grand Prix. Sunday's Grand Prix field is limited to 35 entrants. Those who miss the cut head off to the Sally Hansen Grand Prix on Saturday. The Crown Royal Grand Prix is the Classic's top event, it's $100,000 payoff among the richest on the entire national outdoor circuit. The winnings are sweetened by an additional $75,000 that goes to the rider who can win both the qualifying class and the Grand Prix. (Through 1994, it had yet to be done.)

As mentioned, the Crown Royal is a member of the national Grand Prix League. It is also a qualifying event for the World Cup. A lot is on the line for horse and rider: money, prestige, rank. These incentives, combined with the pure drive of the challenge, are what keep riders and fans alike coming back for more.

Left: *Grand Prix fan favorite Michael Matz introduces The General to a young spectator. Matz went 2-3 in the 1994 Hampton Classic Grand Prix with The General and Olisco.* Opposite: *Grand Prix rider Michael Endicott.*

Hunters

Show riding is essentially divided into two major halves: jumpers and hunters. Jumpers are concerned solely with riding clean rounds. We've covered that. The Hunter Division, along with its sister event Equitation, is also a jumping competition, in the sense that it has jumps. But it is one in which form and style are of utmost importance. Clocks and obstacles do not determine winners. Judges do.

In Hunter classes, judges grade the form and appearance of the horse, whereas Equitation concerns the form and skill of the rider. Hunters must demonstrate smooth jumping ability, an even stride, good manners and a pleasing appearance. Grooming is ultra important. So is a sense of harmony between horse and rider. The more attractive, balanced and graceful the horse, the better the grade on the scorecard. To draw a parallel, the Hunter Division is to figure skating as the jumpers are to speed skating. One is judged, the other is not. One is artistry, presentation and grace, the other is power and speed.

It should be noted that Hunter classes are most akin to the English riding tradition. The obstacles jumped in the ring are made to resemble natural obstacles found in the countryside while on a fox hunt. Along with jumping obstacles, Hunter classes usually require "under saddle" riding, which is work on the flat.

Most hunters are thoroughbreds. In competition, they are divided by experience, size and utility. Working Hunters, for instance, are judged on ability and performance, while Conformation Hunters are judged more for appearance. There are Green Hunters: horses with only one or two years showing experience. There is even a class for ponies.

On top of that, the Hunter Division is broken down by rider. Like the jumpers, there are classes for children, adult amateurs, juniors and amateur-owners.

By far, the Hunter Division draws the most entries at the Hampton Classic. It's no surprise. Most riders compete in this discipline. Plus, the Hampton Classic is one of just six shows in the northeast that is a member event of the American Hunter-Jumper Federation, the group that issues awards both nationally and regionally in virtually every hunter class. The Classic also stages events that are members of the Miller's/Marshall & Sterling Hunter leagues.

Hunter competition at the Classic truly runs the gamut. You've got Green Hunters for starters, both first and second year. First-year horses jump at 3'6", second-year mounts at 3'9". Green Conformation Hunters are divided in the same way, with the judging split just about

evenly between performance and appearance.

Moving up the ladder of experience, you find Regular Working Hunter and Regular Conformation Hunter. These horses, which can be of any age, jump obstacles from 4' to 4'6". (A note: looks aren't as important among the Regular Conformation Hunters as they are with the Greens. Only 25 percent of their grade is on conformation.)

When it comes to out-and-out cuteness, well, who can beat a pony? Ponies are defined as standing no taller than 14.2 hands. At the Classic, the pony field is subdivided by size: Small (12.2 hands or less), Medium (over 12.2, but no bigger than 13.2) and Large (over 13.2, but no bigger than 14.2). Fence heights vary, ranging from 2'3" for Small,

Liz Solter and the famous hunterhorse Rox Dene

2'6" for Medium and 3' for Large. All three feature competition in regular and conformation classes. Each section uses these classes to determine champions. The pony earning the most points, regardless of size, is named Grand Pony Hunter Champ. To cap the week, the Classic runs the $2,500 Pony Hunter Classic.

Now, all Hunter classes mentioned so far are determined by the horse. There are additional sections determined by the rider. The more skilled and experienced riders perform in Regular Working and Conformation Hunter, Junior Working Hunter and Amateur-Owner Working Hunter.

The juniors and amateur-owners, like their jumper brethren, hold separate classes, then combine for the $5,000 Junior/ Amateur-Owner Classic on Sunday. Amateur-owners are divided by age: 18-30 and over-30.

The juniors, riders under the age of 18, are divided by horse size: Large and Small. The top point-getter among the juniors and amateur-owners is named Grand Hunter Champion.

There are also Hunter Division classes for children and adult amateurs. As in the jumpers, these classes are a notch below the junior and amateur-owners. And, like the jumpers, the Children and Adult Amateur Hunter divisions at the Classic are members of the Miller's/ Marshall & Sterling League. Both hold class competition to determine an overall champ, then give all ribbon winners a chance to compete in the $2,500 Children's Hunter Classic and the $2,500 Adult Hunter Classic.

So many events, sometimes nearly not enough time. It is often these classes that you will see riding into the sunset at the Classic.

Equitation

The Show Time spotlight shines last, but not least, on Equitation.

Equitation is a Hunter discipline in the sense that it, too, is judged for style and form. But unlike the Hunter Division, in which the horse is judged, Equitation tests the skill, form and appearance of the rider.

Of the two, Equitation is the more demanding. It forces the rider to adapt to changing courses, something not seen among the hunters, whose courses remain fixed. With changing courses, riders are forced to make dramatic changes in speed, strategy, length of the stride - all while maintaining good balance and handling.

You could say this is much like the changes that jumpers are forced to make in the jump-off. It's a plausible connection. Equitation is a big step into the jumping ring. Some of today's Grand Prix stars first came to prominence as national Equitation champs.

Equitation competition is done both over fences, which entails jumping, and on "the flat," which entails walk, trot and canter demonstrations without jumps. Like the other sections, Equitation competition is divided by age and experience. Maiden Equitation, for instance, is open only to riders who have yet to win a blue ribbon in a recognized show. Novice Equitation is a step up. Riders in this class have won blues, but no more than three.

The best Equitation riding is seen at higher levels. At the Classic, there's plenty of that to go around. That's because the Classic features several major Equitation competitions. Regionally, the Classic is a member event of the Long Island High Score Award Association. It is also a member event of five national competitions: Medal, Maclay, Washington International, PHA and USET. And if that isn't enough, you can add the CK Equitation Championship. This new event, which debuted in 1993, determines the Classic's Equitation champ. It is a very unique event in that the $10,000 purse is divided up among the trainers of the winning riders.

The CK Equitation Championship, sponsored by Calvin Klein (hence the acronym), is a Classic showpiece. It

features riders under the age of 21. It runs in the Grand Prix ring, which gives it the flavor of a big jumping event. So does the two-round format. Riders in the CK Equitation Championship first compete in a qualifying event. The top ten riders come back on Grand Prix Sunday for the final.

While the CK Equitation garners big exposure, the five national events that run at the Classic are of no less importance. Medal and Maclay, the entry-level events in national Equitation competition, involve riders ages 18 and under. Medal and Maclay both culminate in national finals. In Medal, four wins at qualifying events get riders into the finals at Harrisburg, Pennsylvania.

Maclay is a little more involved. Riders must first qualify for regional finals. They do that, at least in the New York area, by winning three qualifying events. The regional finals are held in Port Jervis, a show that follows on the heels of the Classic. Top riders from the regional show advance to the national finals at the National Horse Show in the Meadowlands.

The next step is to move up the national Equitation ladder and compete in the higher events: USET, PHA and Washington International. USET: That's the U.S. Equestrian Team's junior Equitation class. It is open to riders 21 and under. Finals are held in both the East and West. Riders, who compete over fences and on the flat, get into the finals by winning two qualifying events or by amassing 30 points at members shows, such as the

Classic, during the course of the regular season.

The Washington International, the Classic's fourth national Equitation class, is another point-based competition. Member shows are weighted. The bigger the show, the more the points. At the end of the year, the top 25 riders in the point count go to the finals at the Washington International Show.

The Classic's fifth member event is PHA, a class sponsored by the Professional Horsemen's Association. This class does not have a national final, but standings are kept throughout the season. In the

end, the top six riders are honored at the National Horse Show.

Jumper, Hunter, Equitation: These are the major classes that comprise competition at every A-rated horse show. The Classic serves them all up in great heaping portions. Seven days, five rings, 1,300 riders: You will not go home hungry.

Local Day

Each year, the Hampton Classic opens with a phenomenon that has come to be called "Local Day." It falls on the first Sunday of the show and it is the day the rings belong exclusively to horses and riders who either live on Long Island or stable there.

There is a certain symbolism in starting each Classic with the locals. The Classic, after all, grew out of a local show. What better tribute than starting each Classic with a day that captures the essence of those old local shows?

Truth be told, Local Day was not entirely generated by such ideals. It was really the product of numbers. Too many numbers. By 1982, so many Long Island entries were pouring in that Classic organizers decided to set up a special day solely for the locals. And so it has been ever since.

There is one rule governing Local Day. Horses must have been stabled in either Nassau or Suffolk County for at least 75 days of the given year.

While Local Day does feature many horses and riders who compete later in the week, its stated emphasis is noncompetitive. In a way, it is detached from the rest of the show. Local Day is

the only portion of the Classic that is not rated. Fences stand no higher than three feet. Compared to the rest of the show, Local Day is low key.

But don't tell that to the local competitors. Local Day is a big deal for Long Island stables, particularly those in the Hamptons. No matter how involved (or uninvolved) in show riding, all the stables have Local Day circled on the calendar. Reports Wickety Hotchkiss of Stony Hill Stables in Amagansett: "Each year all the parents come and say, 'we want our children to go to the Hampton Classic.' "

Grand Prix star Joe Fargis oversees leadline festivities on Opening Day.

Local Day has an added attraction for stables with low-key operations. By being part of such a prestigious show, Local Day allows them to mingle with the top stars.

"The Hampton Classic is the best show in the country," said Mary Bailey, whose Scuttlehole Farms caters mostly to children. "I like it because there is something for everyone. Here's a show where I can take all these little kids and they can compete at the same place Joe Fargis is riding."

If there is a day for kid riders, Local Day is it. Only on Local Day can you find Short Stirrup and Leadline riding at the Classic. Short Stirrup, an Equitation competition, is for riders ages 12 and under. The leadline riders are even younger, from 3 to 7. Their event is just what the title implies: Little kids on little horses and ponies being led about on a leadline by their handlers. A big deal is made over these little packages. They're a fan favorite, and each year they strut their cute stuff in the Grand Prix ring. Traditionally, Joe Fargis serves as judge.

Local Day also features a veritable feast of regular competition. With the exception of jumpers, most Hunter and Equitation classes are on the menu. In Hunter, locals ride in amateur-owner, junior working and regular working divisions, each of which crowns a champion. There is also a ton of Equitation riding, both among adults and children. There are two events of particular local importance, the Robert Hoskins Junior Medal and the Hugh J.B. Cassidy III Junior Maclay. The top 20 riders for each qualify for the Long Island finals, which are held at the Long Island Classic Horse Show in September.

As for entries, Local Day never lacks. In fact, it just about chokes on the bounty. Over the years, Local Day has been the largest growing segment of the Classic. It's grown so much, said show manager Steve Stephens, that some events had to be spread further into the week. Even with a scaled-back Local Day, the numbers still make it an almost overcrowded day. Some individual classes feature 50-60 riders.

"It's like having three horse shows in one day," states Stephens, who says his most nerve-wracking moments of the week come on Local Day. "I woke up in the morning one year and it was raining. I couldn't take it. I wanted to go home to Florida." No dice Steve. Local Day is here.

Local Day is the hour for Long Island horses and riders to shine.

The World of the Horse

Opening Day is synonymous with Local Day, no doubt about it. But since 1992, Opening Day has also been highlighted by an exhibition called "The World of the Horse." This event, which plays in the Grand Prix ring after the hoopla of leadline, is a tribute to the various breeds and various uses of the horse.

The show has featured an assortment of horses, from miniatures to Arabian stallions to Draft Horses. Invariably, it has featured llamas and alpacas. The exhibit has also featured horses performing in an array of activity, from dressage to polo to police crowd control. The purpose? To showcase horses and activities not normally included at the Classic.

Two groups combine to pull it off. Nine West, the woman's footwear manufacturer, is the presenting sponsor. The show itself is coordinated by the Nassau-Suffolk Horseman's Association.

The World of the Horse emerged as the special event of Opening Day following the demise of the traditional hunt breakfast, in which a fox hunt was recreated in the Grand Prix ring. An Icelandic Horse display filled the gap in 1991 before The World of the Horse debuted the following year.

Nine West stepped into the sponsorship role quite readily. Vince Camuto, the company co-chairman, had been coming to the show regularly to

A member of the Nassau-Suffolk Horsemen's Association, which presents World of the Horse with Nine West.

watch his wife, Kristen, ride. Not only was there a riding connection, but a local one, too. Nine West had recently opened a store in Bridgehampton. With the Classic being a high-profile community event, Nine West jumped at the chance to get involved.

"We got interested in the sport. We think it's a super, en-

ergetic sport for young people, especially young women," Camuto explained. "We just saw the exposure (of the show) and the people who were sponsoring it and thought it would be a good event."

Through the years, The World of the Horse has given spectators the grace and beauty of Icelandic and Arabian horses.

In 1994, fans were treated to a dressage demonstration by Mari Monda Zdnuck and the Andalusian "Loponio IV." The program called it "competitive and école haute dressage." Some spectators called it plain out dancing as, with music playing, Loponio IV sidestepped across the ring, occasionally bowing and going up on his hind legs for a little toe tapping.

The World of the Horse has also served up a slice of Western-style riding. There has been barrel racing, world championship reining. Horses have been shown in practical roles, working crowd control with the cops. Horses have been shown at pure play, in polo and vaulting demonstrations.

While The World of the Horse is a one-day event, many of the participating horses (and llamas) remain on the show grounds for the rest of the week. They can be found in the northwest corner of the Grand Prix ring under the Chaus Exhibition Tent. Several times a day the horses and llamas and ponies are called out for special exhibitions. The Chaus tent also features demonstrations in horse care put on by young riders from local farms. Young, old, big or small, it's all a part of the world of the horse.

Chapter IV: Classic Hoopla

The Show Comes to Town

The sheer scope and size of the show, the large number of events and riders, are enough to make the Hampton Classic the top dog on the national outdoor horse circuit. But there is a whole other dimension to the show that virtually puts the Classic in its own little universe. It is the hoopla that surrounds the show: the fans, the community involvement, the big sponsorships, the celebrities, the media attention.

For those whose sole exposure to show riding comes through the Hampton Classic, all this hoopla is perhaps assumed to be part and parcel to horse shows in general. Well, it's not. People who travel the circuit say the Classic attracts fans, sponsorships and community interest unlike any other American show. In many respects, it's more akin to shows in Europe, where show riding is a veritable Super Bowl.

Reports Ite O'Higgins-Young, a visiting member of the Irish Dressage Team: "In Europe you can't get a ticket to a show. In Dortmund, at seven, eight o'clock in the morning the ring is packed. Everybody comes in: the butcher, the baker, the candlestick maker. It's a big deal. The horse show in Europe is like a big football game in America. At the Hampton Classic, you can't get much better. You can feel the excitement. It was exciting for me because it brought back memories of Europe. It was

This page and overleaf: *Scenes from Bridgehampton, the host community of the Hampton Classic.*

exciting to see something like this happening in America."

According to show estimates, the Classic attracts some 40,000 spectators each year. The show estimated that 20,000 fans watched the 1994 Grand Prix.

All those people can present problems. Once all available parking space is used up - not only on the show grounds, but on neighboring lots - the Classic has no choice but to temporarily close its gates. That's a worry other shows wish they could have.

The crowds are big a the riders revel in the attenti Accustomed to riding mostly der the eye of fellow comp tors, riders at the Classic fi themselves showing in rir circled with spectators. Phot raphers, interviewers are m ing around, too, and it does

ke much cajoling to get Classic
lers, particularly the kids, jun-
rs and amateurs, to field ques-
ns or pose.

"We don't ever have this
ppen to us at other horse
ows," says Good Morning
merica host Joan Lunden,
speaking as a rider, not as an
interviewer (she rides competitively virtually every weekend).
"This show is really in a class of
its own. It's one of the few spec-
tator-oriented shows. This is like
a European show were you have
people pouring in and standing
around the rings. It's an unusual
experience."

"It's almost like a country
fair, as far as the spectators go,"
mused Margo Pachouz, whose
daughter Kara rides with Benchmark Farm in Stamford, Connecticut.

Said John Lytle, a trainer both in Florida and the Hamptons: "The Hampton Classic is unique because it's a social event, a real people-watching event. I don't know of any show, even down in Florida, that draws people like the Hampton Classic."

What brings the people in? For starters, the magnitude of the show itself, both as a sporting and social event. It's the nation's biggest horse show, one that features top riders and horses. Like any other sport, the bigger and better the competition, the bigger the crowd.

On top of that, the Classic plays in a resort community on one of the biggest holiday weekends of the year. The Hamptons are already swarming with Labor Day crowds. The Classic offers a place - and a fashionable one at that - to go.

Indeed, people come to the Classic simply because it is the place to be. The swirl of activity, the horses, the prestige, the celebrity-studded Grand Prix crowd, even the Boutique Garden shopping, make it that way.

"I don't like it as a horse show - I don't ride - I just like it as an event," said Mickey Paraskevas, the artist who produced Classic show posters in 1987 and 1992 as well as the famous Junior Kroll character. "It's a big social event. It's fun to hang out and watch."

Michael Cimino, who directed the movie "The Deerhunter," likens the Classic to other prime events in equestrian sport: the races at Saratoga and Final Days in Cheyenne, the country's oldest rodeo. These are events so big, so tradition-rich, that attendance is almost automatic.

"It's like an eastern version of Final Days at Cheyenne," Cimino said of the Classic. "Wherever people are in the world, they try to make their way back. People just gravitate back. It's something you don't even think about."

Classic organizers must think about attendance, of course, and to that end the show has gone to lengths to promote itself, both locally and to big corporate sponsors.

Don't overlook the local angle. By cultivating local contacts and patrons, the Classic has carved out a foundation other shows don't enjoy. The typical show comes into a town, plays very independently of the surrounding community, then pulls out like a passing night train. The Classic? It has its station.

"It has a place in the community," noted former Olympian and current Grand Prix course designer Conrad Homfeld. "The community is interested in it and comes

Irma Murray: Volunteer

Calling all volunteers.

That's the cry Irma Murray sounds each year when the Classic raises its show tents. Murray is a past president of the Southampton Hospital Auxiliary, which has been providing volunteer workers to the Classic ever since it became a benefit for the local hospital. You could call Murray the ring leader. She took on the task of organizing the volunteer crew back when she was auxiliary president and has kept it even though she no longer holds office.

Spry, good humored and energetic in the pink auxiliary shirt she wears with pride, Murray rounds up some 125-150 volunteers a year to give the Classic a hand. It's a reciprocal deal, really. The hospital saves the Classic some paid staff expenses. The Classic in turn has that much more to donate when the show is over.

Each show day some two dozen hospital volunteers man the spectators gate, Grand Prix tent, reserved ticket gazebo, poster booth and reserve parking lot. Between Opening Day and Friday, 81 working hours are logged daily. The number goes up to 105 hours per day over the weekend. It all adds up to 615 total working hours the Classic does not have to pay for.

"The Classic would have to spend a lot of money to get 150 people and pay them," Murray noted. "The volunteers take this as a dedication, because the hospital benefits."

Murray draws her volunteers from five different auxiliary units that range from Westhampton to Sag Harbor to Montauk. It's a big

Irma Murray has been leading the Southampton Hospital volunteer staff at the Classic since Day 1.

area to canvas, a lot of people. But not everyone volunteers. Fortunately, there is a reliable core that does.

"A lot of people don't like to do this," Murray said. "The people who say yes are dedicated."

There are several "originals" who, like Murray, have been volunteering at the Classic since the beginning. Murray is quick to name Judy Smyzer, Charlotte Holmes, Lyman Babcock, Claudia Cavagnaro, Edith Esp, Marjorie Ludlow and Ida Fisher. These people and all the volunteers put in a lot of hours. But there are some nice perks. While manning the Grand Prix tent over the years, Murray has gotten her picture taken with the likes of former Governor Carey, Peter Jennings, Paul Newman and Joanne Woodward. Hey, you give and you get.

"It's been a joy and I have loved every minute," Murray says. "That's the name of the game."

out and supports it. That's unusual at horse shows."

"This is one of the few
shows that involves the community so much," said Diana De
Rosa, the show's Press Officer.
"I'm sure there are shows out
there that have it, but I don't
know any show that networks
with the community like the
Hampton Classic."

As a show that is run es-
sentially by locals, as one that
benefits the local Southampton
Hospital (and one that provides
a $3 million boost to the regional
economy, according to show estimates), the Classic has always
tapped the resources of the
Hamptons. As we've seen, the
Classic will, in exchange for sign
advertising at the show, bring in
local florists, landscapers and
construction outfits to prepare
the grounds. Southampton Hospital, as the prime beneficiary,
fields some 125 volunteer workers each year.

The Hamptons do turn
out for the Classic. In a resort
that spills over with activity and
hype, the show is one of the big
events of the season, perhaps the
biggest. It's played up that way:
all the promos and souvenirs,
the radio spots and ad campaigns, the TV reports and newspaper coverage. It is the end of
summer in these parts, and it
ensures summer goes out with a
bang.

Under the Big Top

The Hampton Classic is as big a social gala as it is a sporting event. Gilded in Hamptons glitz, the Classic is an established date on the summer party scene. It is traditionally frequented by socialites, celebrities, corporate bigwigs and assorted other lights that sometime seem to overshadow the rest of the show, particularly on Grand Prix Sunday, when the brightest stars come out to play.

The social monster indeed takes on a life of its own at the Hampton Classic, and its nerve center is the Grand Prix Tent. It is where the show's top patrons enjoy lavish catered lunches and ringside seats. It is where the sport's pomp, even aristocratic tradition, is alive and well.

The star-studded social element sets the Classic apart from other horse shows. Yes, those shows have their Grand Prix tents. But, well, they're nothing like this. Said East Hampton realtor Michael Braverman, the host of the Grand Prix Tent, "I've started going to other shows. There are shows with bigger prize money. But there isn't anything so big or beautiful, and there isn't anything with the social aspect this show has, which is found in the Grand Prix Tent."

Who is found in the Grand Prix Tent? On Grand Prix Sunday, the recognizable faces almost certain to be seen are Calvin and Kelly Klein, Peter Jennings, Randy Quaid, Susan Lucci, Tom Wolfe, Peter Boyle and Joan Lunden. Paul Newman and Joanne Woodward, Billy Joel, Billy Baldwin and Stefanie Powers have been known to make an occasional appearance - and that's just a partial list.

Circulating with the celebrities are many top names from the fashion and publishing industries. There are Wall Street wizards and other corporate captains. And, lest we forget that this is a horse show, there are riders, both national and local, along with their farms.

In all, there are 185 tables under that bright white and yellow-striped tent. Those tables can each accommodate 8-15 people as well as a pretty spectacular lunch spread. On Grand Prix Day, each table is packed with both.

The funny thing is, the Classic's Grand Prix Tent hasn't always been a hot spot. In the early years, in fact, the show couldn't give Grand Prix tables away. Nowadays, big dollars compete for those same tables. The list of suitors is long - too long. The Classic must pick and choose. Donations, sponsorships typically decide who gets in.

"We literally used to give these tables away," reported Kelsey Marechal, an original member of the Hampton Classic Board of Directors. "You are now permitted to buy a table. The placement of the table has to do with contribution. The dollar amount of your contribution is not the only thing. You can write all you want, but you won't necessarily get a table unless you're already doing something else."

Securing a table, as Marechal notes, is only half the battle. The jockeying for who sits where is often as competitive as the riding everyone has supposedly gathered to watch.

"I'm afraid so," said Braverman. "Everyone comes to the show, but they're pretty busy with other things. They say there are three competitions: One in the ring, one for the tables and

Foxy Foxy

Margot Horn is the Foxy Lady. She earns the title for the fox logo she uses at her Southampton "We Lead the Hunt" real estate business. Well, there is that thing about the Fox and the Table, too...

Horn has the distinction of being one of the Classic's original sponsors. Since the beginning she has sponsored the Small Junior Working Hunter class.

She has the added distinction of being the only Classic patron to display a stuffed fox on her Grand Prix table. This is a true story. Each year Horn brings an actual stuffed fox to the Classic.

The fox, sad to say, is a glorified road kill. Horn spotted it by the side of the road while driving one day. The little guy was a goner, but his body was still intact. A fox fanatic - the "We Lead the Hunt" office is redolent in fox themes, whether it be in paintings, ornaments or furniture (yes, furniture) - Horn had to stop.

"I knew I'd never be allowed to have a live one, a running one, so I really wanted it," Horn related. "It was sad. Why throw it away?"

Why indeed? But here the first problem presented itself: How to get the critter off the road. Horn asked a passerby for help. Right. "You want it lady," she was told, "you pick it up."

So she did. Then came the next problem. It was Labor Day Weekend. Everything was closed, the local taxidermist included. Where could she store said fox body until it was stuffed? As Horn discovered, there weren't many takers.

Margot Horn's little stuffed fox is the annual centerpiece of the We Lead the Hunt Grand Prix table.

"I called the funeral parlor and they wouldn't take it," Horn recounted. "So I called the meat market. They wouldn't touch it either."

Horn had to rely on her own resources. That meant sacrifices. "I put it in my freezer," she now admits. "I threw away all my mother's Haagen Dazs ice cream."

The fox was eventually stuffed, the ice cream supply replenished. The next issue, and one far more reaching than any of the previous: What to do with a stuffed fox?

Easy. Take it to the horse show. Each year, foxy goes in style to the Classic. Crowned by a top hat, the fox is the centerpiece of Horn's table, where she entertains friends. This is one of two parties Horn puts on each year. The other is her mother's birthday party.

"I find it a great place to give a party, because after my guests have finished their lunch and chatting up my table they can visit and chat up other tables," Horn says of her Classic bash. "They never have so much amusement if they're horse people. If they're not horse people, if they don't like anything about horses, if they can't stand the smell of them, they can come to mother's party."

one for what happens under the tent."

"It takes on a life of its own," Braverman added. "I think it happens because a lot of people in here, at least on Grand Prix Day, have one eye on the horses and one eye on who's at the next table."

How did the Grand Prix Tent become such a phenomenon? The Hamptons location had a lot to do with it. So did the boom times of the 80's, which really kicked the ritzy Hamptons scene into overdrive by bringing in new money - money that gladly took itself out to the horse show in a way the old money did not. ("The old money in the Hamptons doesn't spend money at the events," said Braverman.)

Perhaps the biggest key of all: The Classic became trendy. It started with a ripple from people already involved with riding. Calvin Klein came out to watch his wife Kelly, who is a rider. While still married, Billy Joel and Christie Brinkley were regulars, she being very much interested in riding. They were joined by a group of celebrities whose children caught the riding bug. Paul Newman and Joanne Woodward, Peter Boyle, Peter Jennings, Tom Wolfe and Joan Lunden all have children who ride regularly at the Classic, as well as other shows. Lunden, for that matter, is a rider in her own right. Randy Quaid's wife Evi rides. The basic connection of these people to

the Classic was fairly pedestrian. Yet the prestige of their names lured the others in. It was pure bees to honey. "Once you get a few big names it's almost automatic all the others follow," Braverman observed. They did follow. The Classic estimates that each year more than 2,000 patrons squeeze under the tent on Grand Prix Sunday.

Atmosphere and attendance do vary under the big top during the week. Opening Day is given over to sponsoring corporations and the locals. The place is full, yet a mere shadow of what's to come a week later. Weekdays are relaxed, even low key. If you're a patron truly into show riding, the week's the time to come. The tent is comfortable, quiet (virtually media-free) and the riding is the same.

The peace starts to shatter on Saturday as patrons come in for the weekend. On Sunday, it is obliterated amid the popping of camera flashes and champagne corks. The photogs, some of whom have slipped security, spot a famous face and descend in a burst of halogen. The aisles are cloaked in suits and ties, designer dresses, designer hats. The tables are overloaded with food. There is so much wealth on display, so much prestige. And yet there is this mania, this sense of uncontrollable and even desperate release. The cynic might say that. Others just call it Classic magic.

"Just something happens in the air on Grand Prix Day," Braverman mused. "It's hard to put into words. It's something that doesn't happen at other shows and doesn't happen at other social events. It's definitely here. Anything associated with the Classic takes on that magic."

"There's this tremendous energy, yet there's this calm. The space and beauty of the show gives it the calm. At the same time, you can take three tables and eliminate the deficit."

Indeed, as much as it is a day in the country, Grand Prix Sunday is a business opportunity. Braverman knows it. He's away from the office during the Classic. But he's not exactly on vacation. There are contacts to be cultivated under that tent, deals to be had. Martha Stewart attended Grand Prix Day one year. The very next morning she was on the phone to Braverman in search of a Hamptons home.

"In my view, it's very important for business," Braverman said. "I try to become the broker most associated with the show."

"It would be easy to exceed the $1.75 million gross of the show with the private deals that are made in here in the course of the week," Marechal speculated.

It could be said the Grand Prix Tent is like a Monopoly board. Some spaces are more desirable than others. For starters, the Grand Prix Tent must be distinguished from the U.S. Equestrian Team tent. The Grand Prix runs east-west, the USET north-south. The Grand Prix is considered the more prestigious of the two, sort of the Pacific Ave-Boardwalk strip.

The USET tent, though, is probably the more comfortable,

Watchdogs at the Gate

Gate crashing is the biggest headache the Classic encounters each year with the Grand Prix Tent. Everybody wants to get in, not everyone can. No wristband - it's amazing how valuable a little strip of plastic can become - means no entry.

Not that that stops anyone from trying. "Nobody has a ticket, but everybody has a story," sighs Michael Braverman, the host of the Grand Prix Tent. "They all claim they are someone or know someone."

Grand Prix security has heard it all, no doubt. Still, the guards must stay sharp, and they seem to do it with great firmness and alacrity. Anyone caught inside the big top without a pass can vouch for that. "It was suggested we go to a medium-security prison and get a job there," Braverman says with a smile.

You could say some gate guards take their job more seriously, more literally than others. You could count local show official Barbara Topping in that group.

Calvin Klein could tell you. One year he showed up on Grand Prix Day without his pass. Topping wouldn't budge. Klein, one of the Classic's biggest sponsors, dropped his name. That didn't help either, which prompted the Mickey Paraskevas "I Don't Care If Your Name Is Calvin Klein" cartoon.

To make sure this sort of incident would not repeat itself, Classic organizers gave Topping a few extra passes the following year. "These are the spares," she was told.

Naturally, the same scenario came to pass: Klein showed up sans pass; Topping refused to let him in. No doubt the $25,000 Calvin Klein Show Jumping Derby was playing in the Grand Prix Ring at the very moment.

Executive Director Jean Lindgren was called in to mediate. Arriving, she pointed to the box of extra passes. "Why didn't you give him one of these?" she asked Topping. Straightfaced, Topping replied, "those are for the Spare family."

Pass or no pass: Michael Braverman and several hospital volunteers man the gate.

being more sheltered from the wind, and the view is just as good. It's like the Kentucky Ave-Marvin Gardens wing: Good return on the investment. It breaks down further. Within the tents are divisions of desirability. The Grand Prix Tent, for instance, has two tiers. One faces the Grand Prix ring, the other the back jumper ring. It's easy to imagine which costs the prettier penny.

What is the choicest spot of all? The Boardwalk of the Classic? Dead center in the Grand Prix tent. This spot is akin to the 50-yard-line seat. Here you will find Calvin and Kelly Klein, Classic President Dennis Suskind and his family. Celebrities and other top sponsors are in the immediate vicinity. More corporate honchos, the entire Board of Directors is spread throughout. Most of the horse people gather near the east end of the Grand Prix Tent. That allows for an easy exit to the show rings.

They're all in there, in where you can't go unless you have a coveted pass. Each year the head count is pegged at 2,000-plus, and as the show zooms deeper into the 90's toward its third decade, there seems to be no let up. Nor is there fear the Grand Prix rose will fade. Grand Prix Sunday comes but once a year, so it's hard to overplay. Plus, the Classic keeps making the trip out east worthwhile.

"The show, incredibly, just gets better," said Braverman. "It's sort of earned its place, that it will always be a part of the Hamptons and the communities."

Michael Braverman fields a confidential request. Movie director Michael Cimino is in the background.

Calvin Klein and Bianca Jagger were among the famous faces on a recent Grand Prix Sunday (photo courtesy of Hampton Classic).

Consequently, it attracts "Lifestyles of the Rich and Famous." People, Vogue, Harper's Bazaar, Town & Country, the New Yorker and Women's Wear Daily have also chronicled the social aspects of the show.

Some media outlets take it a step farther and sponsor the Classic. Harper's Bazaar and Town & Country both sponsor events. Spur is a big advertiser. So is the Hamptons' local Dan's Papers. Newsday, the Long Island daily, became a sponsor in 1994.

All the attention makes the Classic the most thoroughly covered horse show in the country. The show's sports/Hollywood East duality, Hamptons' mystique and New York market combine to make it that way. None of the other shows even come close.

"A lot of events just get equine coverage," said De Rosa, who has covered Olympics and World Equestrian championships.

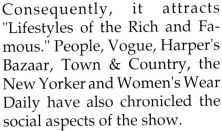

Some of the Locals. Top left: *Charlie Styler of Channel 27.* Top right: *Jack Graves of the East Hampton Star.* Above: *The Big Man, Roger Molter, from Sag Harbor's WLNG.*

Tables turned: Good Morning America host and weekend show rider Joan Lunden gets on the other side of the mike at the Hampton Classic.

"This is an event that has more open doors - to the social media, to the entertainment media."

The latter groups contribute heavily to the media hysteria that descends on Grand Prix Sunday. The social/entertainment outlets, the paparazzi, want a good peek at the Grand Prix Tent action. The result, at times, has been chaos and ruffled feathers. Most celebrities don't want to be bothered at the show.

As a result, press access to the Big Top has been curtailed. Yet at the same time, the show doesn't want to shut it off completely. Exposure, after all, is exposure, and exposure has helped the show go big time.

Obviously, the most lucrative media channel has been television. The Classic made its television debut in 1986 with ESPN. Back then, the Classic paid for airtime. Times have changed. Nowadays, the show fields bids from prospective televisors. It has its own television coordinator in David Hoffman.

Most recently, the Classic has been televised by Yorkshire Television America, a division of the British-based ITV. According to Monica de Hellerman, the executive vice president of York-

shire Television America, the telecast was distributed worldwide to countries from Sri Lanka to Chile. In America, the show could be seen on Prime Network.

The potential audience: 28 million homes, and that's just counting the U.S. That's a lot of eyes, and when it comes to the Classic, the eyes are watching.

Media Beat. Top left: *Marty Bauman.* Top right: *Photogs at the ready to capture leadline.* Bottom left: *The pack interviews 1994 Grand Prix champ Jeffrey Welles.* Bottom right: *Press Officer Diana De Rosa.*

Boutique Garden

In our great mall culture, what would any event be without shopping?

The Hampton Classic is hardly immune to the big sell. Shopping is a big part of the Classic experience for many who come through the gates. Buying the new Classic poster, picking up a shirt: This can be as integral as going to the show itself.

The great Classic marketplace is the Boutique Garden. Located before the spectator entry to the Grand Prix ring, the Garden features 30 shops tucked in 10x10 stalls aligned around an open square. Nearly 20 other shops are lined up along Stable Lane, which extends away from the main Garden and faces the stabling area. Goods are crammed inside the stalls; goods spill out the front in enticing displays. Combined, the entire Boutique comes off like coral: each year it seems one notch bigger.

Name it and you can probably buy it at the Classic. There are dealers peddling hats, boots, clothes, leather goods, antiques, jewelry, equestrian equipment, equestrian art, equestrian photography.

The tastes, the styles run toward the high end. So do the prices. For $300 you've got a designer hat for Grand Prix Sunday. A mere $400 can put a snakeskin belt around your waist (which no doubt will be shrinking now that you have no food money).

The Boutique Garden is not unique to the Classic. Most shows have one. Many have the same exhibitors. These are merchants who deal in equestrian-related trades or fashions. They travel the show circuit right along with the riders and farms.

At the Classic, the Boutique Garden emerged much like the Grand Prix Tent. What once couldn't be given away is now filled to the brim. The Boutique cup overflows, in fact. There are far more applicants than accommodations. Who gets in? Usually only the best. The Classic likes to go with the top-line outfits. The price? A $1,200 entry fee and an obligatory ad in the show program. "Everybody tries to get into this show," reported Tracey Tooker of the eponymous hat shop. "It's one of the best shows."

The traditional exhibitors at the Classic are the circuit riders: Henry Vogel's boot supply, Bob Ermilio's tailor shop, to name a few. These are businesses that spend much of the year on the road - "we're gypsies," Ermilio says - because it is most lucrative to stay in steady touch with the ready-made customer base. Vogel, for instance, supplies boots to Grand Prix riders, not to mention the U.S., English, Dutch and French equestrian teams.

Mobility has its rewards. Boutiques open shops to new customers show after show, state after state. The sale isn't so much the thing as the exposure. "This is important," remarked Henry Vogel. "It puts you in front of the public. The shows are generally nice. The people come out, but they may not necessarily want to sit around all day and watch horses. This is a good diversion to buy some quality goods."

Who's selling? Some fairly impressive names.

In 1994, the Classic welcomed Frost & Reed Limited of London, the Old Bond Street gallery considered to be the premier equestrian art exhibitor and dealer in the world. A traditional exhibitor at Saratoga, Frost & Reed wanted to make the Classic part of its stateside tour. The Classic follows right on the heels of the races, so the timing was good. In its first year in the Hamptons,

Frost & Reed brought in works from Munnings, Aiken, Fatin-Latour, even Renoir. Many were in original frames. They were also for sale. A Fatin-Latour piece occupied the high end at $700,000. A $45,000 Degas was the bargain item. The total inventory: $3.5 million.

"There aren't many people who can put three and a half million in merchandising in a tent, or would want to," remarked Frost & Reed director A.G. Nevill, who, despite the trusty vigilance of Classic security, wisely took his wares off the lot each night.

The 1994 show also featured Wathne, the sports fashion company. Though a long-running sponsor of the Classic, that year marked Wathne's first in the Boutique Garden. It was part of Wathne's public emergence. Traditionally a catalog company, Wathne established its flagship store in October of 1994 on New York's 57th Street. The Boutique was a dry run, if you will.

"We thought we would try it and see how it worked for us," said Carol Kingston, Wathne's PR director. "We were

a catalog company for so long we thought it would be good to bring the business to the people who might not know about us."

Who else do Classic shoppers know? They may recognize the face of Bob Ermilio, the tailor from suburban Philadelphia who's been at the Classic each year since the 1980's. They may not know that it was his shop that created the famous green Masters golf jacket. That was in 1942, when Ermilio's father ran the store. The family business goes back even further, back to 1904 when Ermilio's

grandfather established himself. Along the way, Ermilio's has outfitted thousands, including former President Dwight Eisenhower and Grace Kelly.

The Hampton Classic has clothed a few people in its own right, no doubt some of them famous. By far the busiest corner of the Boutique Garden is the one occupied by the Hampton Classic souvenir shop. There you'll find parents and kids queueing up for Hampton Classic shirts, jackets, hats, mugs, umbrellas, bags and anything else that can accommodate the show logo.

What's your fancy? The styles vary. You can get a t-shirt for as low as $10, a zip-neck hooded sweater for $65 (1994 prices). Maybe you'd like a drawstring jacket ($50) or a wool coat ($150). Maybe you'd just like to go see for yourself.

What's the best day to shop? Vendors report that they see a lot of business during the week. While Grand Prix Sunday draws the biggest crowds, it's not necessarily the best business day because most spectators are occupied with the Grand Prix.

All in all, dealers count the Classic as a prime stop on the boutique tour because the Classic draws crowds like no other show. It's a big crowd, a Hamptons crowd with handsome dollars - dollars that come through the front gate and often never make it to the Grand Prix ring.

Boutique Garden exhibitors at the 1994 Classic included (top) Barbara Blumberg and Wathne and (bottom) tailor Bob Ermilio.

Classic Art

An overview of the Hampton Classic would be incomplete without a little art and art history.

This has nothing to do with the artistry of horse and rider -though there is plenty of that- but with posters. Since 1978, the Hampton Classic has run an annual poster to promote the show. The tradition actually started in 1976 at the Southampton Horse Show with a Joseph Cornell piece owned by organizer Marie-Christophe de Menil.

That set the trend. In the years since, the poster series has produced some memorable pieces, some experimental ones. It's also produced some revenue for the show. And, no matter what your taste, the posters have produced a whole other dimension to the Hampton Classic. They stand as the visual stamp of each show.

As the Classic has evolved, so has the poster series. It started out as a joint venture with a New York poster firm. Under the arrangement, the firm produced the poster, gave several hundred copies to the Classic and retained the rights to the rest.

This worked well enough for the Classic in the early years. The fledgling show took on no financial risk. But drawbacks became evident. The New York firm had a big influence over which artists and pieces were selected. There was also a little lucrative business at hand that

A Classic Original: Paul Davis, designer of the Hampton Classic logo and first Classic poster, at his home in Sag Harbor.

the Classic felt it shouldn't be missing out on.

Thus, in 1985 the Classic took over sole production of the poster. An art committee was appointed to handle the chore. Each spring, the committee meets to wade through submissions and pick the definitive piece. Sometimes artists are asked to produce a work. Preference is given to local artists.

The whole operation has come a long way. Nowadays, the Classic poster, fueled by a national distribution system, nets some $20,000 a year.

"Through the years it's turned out quite well," said Bridgehampton gallery owner

Elaine Benson, the chairman of the Classic poster committee. "And to make that kind of money? In the beginning we never thought it would happen. The posters have become more than advertising. They sort of give a flavor to the show."

An acrylic painting of an English-style rider by Paul Davis opened the series in 1978. It is the most recognizable of the set. Each year, it adorns the front cover of the show program. Since then, the Classic series has featured an array of styles, from the realism of Henry Koehler to the illustrations of Mickey Paraskevas to the experimentation of Robert Weaver. The variety was intentional. The poster committee looks for diversity as it combs through the 20 to 30 submissions it receives each year. Offbeat, yet topical work is a plus. The predictable, the common is dismissed.

"We try to come up with something greatly different from the year before," said Benson. "There tends to be a sameness because people come to the Classic and do sketches and take them home. So we're always looking for anything that is offbeat."

That's fine. But a poster obviously needs to be more. It has to bridge between the art world and the equestrian world. It has to be a good piece of art to satisfy the artists and it has to be technically correct, in terms of tack and uniform, to satisfy the horse people. (Both groups are represented on the poster committee.) On top of that, the piece has to work well as a poster.

"It's one thing to translate a painting into a poster, it's another to understand conceptually what will work graphically and translate to the viewer's eye," Benson said. "You can be the best artist or illustrator and not be able to do a great poster."

The Classic series has featured the work of painters, sketchers, illustrators. Of the lot of them, the illustrators wax most philosophical about the purpose of the poster. "A poster should be a strong image that tells a little bit of the story or piques one's interest in the event," said Lauren Jarrett, the East Hampton illustrator who did the 1984 Classic poster. "A poster has to talk a bit."

Room with a View: Southampton painter Henry Koehler has produced an unmatched three Classic posters.

"I like to do something which is fairly rich narratively to give the viewer a certain amount of detail, but to really make it a poster," said James McMullen, the illustrator of the 1982 poster. "A poster needs to be simplified. It's supposed to be something you see out in the world en route to some place else. So it should read relatively fast. If you make it too complete, it seems like the experience."

Hampton Classic art actually existed before there was a poster series or even a Hampton Classic. Most of the early works had been completed long before they were reinvented as horse show posters.

Left: *Realist painter Albert Sharp was unhappy with the way his 1980 poster was reproduced; he'd love a second crack.* Right: *Illustrator James McMullen found his equestrian inspiration in Pennsylvania.*

The pioneer poster, Paul Davis's English rider, was first used as the cover design for the Southampton Horse Show's 1971 program. On his way to a successful career as an illustrator in magazines and for Joe Papp's Shakespeare Festival (among other endeavors), Davis was asked to do the piece by Maria (Koenig) Matthiessen. A show organizer, Maria wanted the show program to have some quality. The finished product, a 5x7 book, turned out to be an advertising-laden guide that is arguably the forerunner of the modern Hampton Classic program.

For one thing, the cover is still the same. Davis's now familiar English rider in blue coat and tan breeches is set against a soft white cloud in a light blue sky. Here's a secret: the model was a daughter of Bud and Tinka Topping, who were hosting the Southampton Horse Show at the time at Topping Riding Club.

The cover painting was also used as a poster, though much was lost in the reproduction, which was done all in brown. The painting was reproduced in its original color when used for the Hampton Classic in 1978. (A note: the debut poster contained a typo. The headline reads "Hamptons Classic.") The Davis piece is a trademark of sorts for the Hampton Classic, given its annual appearance on the program cover. But this should not be confused with the show's official trademark, which is a circular stamp containing the silhouette of a horse and rider. Davis designed that as well.

Another one of the Classic's more famous poster artists appeared on the scene in 1979: Henry Koehler. Over the next 15 years, the Southampton painter would produce three Classic posters. This sort of work was right up Koehler's alley. Many of his themes are sports related. His first big commission came from Sports Illustrated, which assigned him to cover a sailing regatta off San Diego. On top of that, Koehler's particular interest lay in equestrian themes. As his career grew - the painter would hold more than 50 one-man exhibitions - Koehler drew the patronage of the famous. The list included the Prince of Wales and First Lady Jacqueline Kennedy.

The Classic folks liked his work, too, and in 1979 they chose one of his pieces for their poster. It was an oil painting of a female rider in red. Viewed from the side, she is seen in the saddle, reaching over and patting the side of a white horse. Koehler says the painting became a poster by accident. It was, he said, a last-minute selection.

A Koehler piece would next appear on a Classic poster in 1985. In the meantime, 1980 saw a production that pleased few involved. This was the first year in which a work was done specifically for the poster. The appointed artist was East Hampton painter Albert Sharp. A painter of pastoral landscapes in the French tradition, Sharp's attention to detail is meticulous. For the poster, Sharp produced a piece showing mares and foals standing outside a show tent. The details were distinct. But the poster was produced in only two tones, first in black and white, then in brown and peach. Sharp was unhappy. All the detail was lost, he said. The final result looked more like a photo negative than a painting.

Full-fledged color returned in 1981 with a painting by Richard Mantel. This would be the first of two Classic posters for the New York artist. The first looked much like the Paul Davis piece. It too featured an English rider mounted on a horse before a light blue background, though this rider was a man in a red coat and top hat.

In 1982, the Classic turned to illustrator James McMullen. Like Davis, McMullen had come out of New York's Push Pin Studio. Posters were his forte. In time, he would do dozens of posters for theatrical works at Lin-

coln Center. He would also keep busy locally with the Hampton Library poster series. In '82, Jean Lindgren asked him to do the Classic poster. Not satisfied with the photographs Lindgren had provided him for possible themes, McMullen headed out to Pennsylvania for a little first-hand experience at the Devon Horse Show. There, he found his inspiration - not in what went on in the ring, but in what went on outside it.

"I went to the top of the bleachers," McMullen related. "I looked behind me and saw all these people and horses circling around and getting ready to enter the ring."

The group scene was duplicated in McMullen's poster. It was the first of its kind in the Classic series. Some half dozen horses are seen in varying states

of preparation. A groom is leading in one horse. A rider, mounted on another, is adjusting his cap. Blue and gray are the prevalent tones, a reflection of an overcast day at Devon. "The picture was very intriguing and that led me to a very flat vision of horses on a gray day," McMullen said. "I'm sure the gray day led to the blues in my painting."

The overcast tones of McMullen's piece gave way to the sunny quality of Susan Slyman's 1983 painting. It's a folksy piece, revealing a show in microcosm: a busy ring in the foreground, spectators and vendors in the background, all on a bright day in the country.

The bright tones continued in 1984, when East Hampton illustrator Lauren Jarrett was called on to do a piece. An illustrator of cookbooks, garden books and posters, Jarrett found

A non-horse person, East Hampton illustrator Lauren Jarrett took her cue from dressage.

Henry Koehler returned to the Classic poster series in 1985 with a unique still life.

inspiration in dressage. To capture the dancing movement of the sport, Jarrett did a series of pictures of the same horse and rider and ran them together in three tiers.

"I had to come up with something, not being a horse person, that appealed to me as a visual image," Jarrett recalled. "What I liked was the repetition, precision and beauty of dressage. It was a chance to do something sequential. I wanted a prancing feel to it. The way I thought to show that moving image was to have three bands of activity."

Jarrett's "motion" piece was the first of its kind for the Classic. So was the poster that followed in 1985. It was the second of Koehler's three Classic works and it remains the most unique of the whole series. It's a tasty mood piece, a still life of boots and caps and a red riding jacket all set before a window. No horses, no riders, but so evocative of the quiet majesty of

riding. For Koehler, who serves on the poster committee, it was merely a different way to capture the essence of the show. "I do a lot of sport still lifes," Koehler said. "I don't think you always have to do a scene at the horse show."

This Koehler piece, a pre-existing work not done specifically for the show, was the first poster the Classic produced on its own. It was also the first poster to produce "offshoot" memorabilia - in this case, postcards. In time, poster images would also adorn T-shirts.

The 1985 poster was truly a breakthrough, both in design and production. Then came 1986 and a poster that was, well, a conversation piece. It was, some say, a poster you either loved or loathed. Count us in the former camp. The poster is a reproduction of a painting done by New York's John Register. It is an extreme close up of a horse going over a jump, though the jump

itself is not seen because the view is from ground level looking up. Also out of sight is the top half of the rider and the hindquarters of the horse. Painted in broad strokes in purples and browns, it is without question the most "painterly" (Benson's term) poster in the series.

The 1987 poster introduced Classic fans to the work of Mickey Paraskevas, the Jersey guy who would gain renown for his magazine illustrations and a little thing called Junior Kroll, the bowl-cut kid Mickey created to illustrate a popular series written by his mother Betty. Mickey's 1987 work was the first of two posters he would do for the Classic. His ubiquitous sketchbook is what got him in the door. The previous year, a friend had taken him to the show. Though not a horse person, Paraskevas was immediately hooked. He wound up filling a whole set of sketchbooks. They were shown to Tony Hitchcock and Jean Lindgren. Impressed, the Classic directors signed him up for the following year. Paraskevas initially wanted to do one sketch, but wound up going with four - another Classic first.

Paraskevas got more involved with the show, eventually becoming a member of the poster committee. Each year he takes his vacation when the Classic is in town. He hangs out the whole week, drawing and taking in the ambience of the show. He is, as he puts it, as sketchbook journalist, capturing the minutiae that adds up to the Classic.

A Paraskevas sketch of a group of horses and riders made it to the Classic poster in 1992. Mickey's standing on the poster

Mickey Paraskevas has, eh hem, made a splash on the Classic poster series and with Junior Kroll.

committee also made him instrumental in the 1989 poster. He solicited the work of his teacher, Robert Weaver. The resulting product was much like the Register piece of 1986. You either loved it or loathed it. The most experimental in the series, the poster is a collage of a horse and rider. Laid against olive green fabric, the horse is comprised of pieces pinned together. The rider is taken from a photograph and superimposed over the horse.

Weaver's piece followed on the heels of the more conventional poster in 1988. That was Nina Duran's painting of a scene that is clearly taken from the Classic and no place else. The view is from the rear. A horse is seen going over a wagon wheel jump.

Striped tents of blue, yellow and white loom in the background. A little white dog sniffs about in one of the lower corners. It was pure Classic - the view is from the Grand Prix Tent looking back over the Jumper Ring, to be exact. Because of that familiarity, it was extremely popular.

Following the Weaver experiment of 1989, the poster committee returned to traditional ground in 1990 with another painting from Mantel. This piece was much like the first: a single rider on a single horse set against a light blue background. The poster showed a woman sitting side saddle, her long red dress blooming against the brown of her horse. It was straightforward; it was familiar.

Jamesport painter Lynn Curlee.

The other posters of the early 90's featured a newcomer and an old hand. Lynn Curlee, a painter out of Jamesport, cracked into the series in 1991 with an acrylic painting of a rider coming straight on over a Swedish gate. The work is perfectly symmetrical. That's a Curlee trademark. "Symmetry is highly underestimated," the artist said. "A lot of painters shy away from it. It's considered too simplistic, too rigid. But these can be virtues."

After showing the previous winter at Elaine Benson's gallery and finding out how the poster selection worked, Curlee produced his painting specifically for a Classic poster. He made his submission, and the committee went with it. The equestrian theme was something of a new theme for Curlee, but that in itself was nothing new.

His paintings and book illustrations cover a wide range, from portraits to animals to sailing to mythological figures to dirigibles. Another thing about Curlee: he works large. Most of his paintings are done on immense canvasses. The original for the Classic poster measured 4x4 feet. Paraskevas, whose second Classic work followed in 1992, is just the opposite. In some of his pocket-sized books, sketches measure 4x4 inches.

In 1993, the Classic leaned on old familiar Henry Koehler. This, his third poster, was the only one he did expressly for the show. It was another oil, this time in a rich golden hue, that portrayed a child rider amid a background of other horses and riders. To maximize attention on that child, the heads of the other figures, including that of an adult

in the foreground, run off the top edge. The painting was submitted as part of an eight-piece series. All eight featured children. "There have been a lot pictures of people jumping, a lot of the glamor part," Koehler said. "But the backbone of the show is the kids. So I said let's do one that involves children."

Children, group scenes, single rider, even a doctored horse held together by pins: The themes have roamed with little repetition. In 1994, the 18th Classic poster, done by upstate artist Patricia Powers, featured yet another new scene: a riderless horse standing majestically before an arch. The ideas, the posters never seem to get old. In many respects, they've gotten to be the one thing people first look for at the show, appetizers that set the flavor of what's to follow.

Chapter V: The Locals

The Local Evolution

No matter how big it gets, no matter how far-reaching, the Hampton Classic can not escape its local roots.

The Classic, as we've seen, grew out of the Southampton Horse Show, a Hamptons' event that dated back to the turn of the century. Since its formal establishment in 1977, the Hampton Classic has grown into the largest outdoor horse show in America. The locals helped get it there. They were the ones who conceived the idea and, with some help, brought it to fruition. In turn, the locals saw their once little world of riding blossom into prominence.

It's all too clear. The rise of the local scene has paralleled the rise of the Classic. What was once home to a handful of small stables running small lessons and small unrecognized shows has steadily broadened into a veritable universe that features more than a dozen stables and a galaxy of A-rated shows. And it's all happened in the last 25 years.

Nowadays, the lineup of Hamptons' stables features a diverse mix. There are barns big into show riding - barns that offer extensive lesson programs and travel regularly on the show circuit. Topping Riding Club in Sagaponack and Swan Creek Farms in Bridgehampton, two of the original Hampton stables, are among that crowd, as are riders who train in the summer in Water Mill with independent guru Charlie Weaver. Sag Pond Farm in Sagaponack, Two Trees Stables in Water Mill and little Applewild Farm in Bridgehampton are among the relative new faces striking out for big-time show riding.

Other local barns dabble in show riding, but on a limited scale - places like Clearview in Southampton and Scuttlehole Farms in Water Mill. Those farms, like others who show more frequently - Stony Hill Stables in Amagansett, Hillcrest Farm in Riverhead and East End Stables in East Hampton, to name a few - are big into lesson programs, pony camps and the like.

The Hamptons riding scene truly runs the gamut, from big to small. One of the smaller barns, ironically, is run by two of the bigger names in American show riding. They are Joe Fargis and Conrad Homfeld, the former U.S. Olympians and Hampton Classic Grand Prix winners who operate Sandron, a strictly private barn, in Southampton. And, in keeping with Hamptons' celebrity chic, there is even a barn owned by an actress: Stephanie Powers' Five Tails Farm in Bridgehampton.

Some Hamptons' stables are bigger than others, some more serious. Some draw a well-to-do clientele, others draw from the middle of the road. Ultimately, though, they are alike. They all call the East End home and, when the magic date in late summer rolls around, they all love to ride at the Hampton Classic on Local Day. The local riding scene has truly gone big time. Here's how it got there.

* * * *

Given its agricultural heritage, horses have always been a part of the East End. Horses pulled the plows that tilled the fields. Horses served as transportation. As for show riding, that dimension began making its appearance in the Hamptons around the turn of the century, when the area was blossoming as a resort community. High society folk would bring their horses out for the summer. They formed hunt clubs. One, the Southampton Riding and Hunt Club, hosted the Southampton Horse Show during the 1920's. and 1930's.

Interest in riding and hunting also circulated among local folk and others outside the upper caste. These people were home-grown operators for the most part. They kept their horses in small stables in the backyard. Bona fide horse farms didn't really come into being on the East End until the 1950's. In 1954, Elizabeth Hotchkiss established Stony Hill Stables in Amagansett. Still operating 40 years later under Elizabeth's daughter Wickety, Stony Hill is the oldest stable in continuous operation in the Hamptons.

Back then, there were other small stables like Stony Hill that gave lessons, mostly to kids who came out for the summer. They even held a few small shows. But these operations were thor-

Fox hunting at Swan Creek Farms, Bridgehampton, 1973. (Photo courtesy Patsy Topping.)

Patsy Topping of Swan Creek Farms (above), one of the East End equestrian originals, has seen the Hamptons emerge as prime show riding country.

oughly small time, especially when compared to today. Even the society folk, who carried on with the Southampton Horse Show and their private clubs, would have seemed backyard by today's standards. Their trainers would be considered little more than glorified grooms today.

There was another key difference between then and now. In the old days, horses were multi-purpose. Horses used in the show ring in the summer were taken out on the fox hunt in the winter. That changed in the mid-1960's when several top-flight riders opened barns in different parts of the country to expressly train show horses. In essence, this was the Great Schism of show riding. Horses, the better ones at least, became specialty items. They were trained specifically for show riding.

This, in turn, changed the whole nature of horse shows. Hitherto, shows had been more social event than sporting event. Now, the competition became the key. Training became a science. The upshot was predictable. Bigger barns started popping up in the metropolitan area. The wave steadily spread eastward across Long Island throughout the rest of the 60's. By the end of the decade, two new stables joined the ranks of Stony Hill: Bud and Tinka Topping's Topping Riding Club (1968) and Alvin and Patsy Topping's Swan Creek (1970). All of these stables were relatively small operations. They gave lessons, offered trail rides. These farms, along with an East Hampton stable run by Sue Marder, also held shows. They were small, unrecognized shows. Contributing to the smallness of these

shows was the fact that they were held independently of one another.

That changed in the early 70's when the four shows banded together. The result was the Hampton High Score Series. Each farm continued to host its own show, but now all four were intertwined. Results carried from show to show and were used to determine overall champions. The Hampton High Score Series, though short-lived, was a glimpse of the spirit that would lead to the Hampton Classic: Local stables pooling their resources to form a larger, more ambitious event.

The locals were truly moving up. In the early 70's the annual show at Topping Riding Club, the Sagaponack Horse Show, was used to revive the

Southampton Horse Show, which had been defunct for several years. In absorbing the old Southampton event, the Sagaponack show, a yearly benefit for the private Hampton Day School, was recognized by the American Horse Shows Association. Around the same time, Swan Creek landed a recognized event with the Ladies Village Improvement Society Show.

All this led to the big breakthrough. The year was 1976 and the Southampton Horse Show, at the suggestion of Sag Harbor rider Marie-Christophe de Menil, took on an A-rated status by expanding from a one-day show to a five-day event. That was the move that led to the official emergence of the Hampton Classic.

It was a move that also changed the face of riding in the Hamptons. The cause and effect was pretty basic. With the A-rated Classic, the Hamptons had a longer show and a show with more classes and prize money. With a better show, the Hamptons drew better horses and better riders. Some began bringing their horses out East for the summer. As the competition improved, local riders felt obligated to keep pace. They bought better horses; they demanded better training. Local stables responded.

"We had the recognized shows and people had the desire to improve," said Swan Creek's Patsy Topping. "So, yes, we evolved very quickly. By 1977, 1978, we had a team of 15 to 20 horses that were competitive at every show but the Hampton Classic. At the Hampton Classic we'd say if we get a few ribbons

Olympic Connection

For a little corner of the world, the Hamptons own a nice collection of Olympic equestrian hardware.

Riders and horses familiar to the East End of Long Island were part of the glory in the 1980's and 90's when American Olympians made in-roads into a sport traditionally dominated on the international level by Europeans. East Enders were members of United States Equestrian teams that, starting in 1984, won medals in three straight Summer Olympics.

Joe Fargis and Conrad Homfeld, the operators of the Southampton farm Sandron, headlined America's glittering performance in show jumping at the 1984 Summer Olympics in Los Angeles. Fargis became only the second American ever to win an individual show jumping gold when he guided "Touch of Class" to first place. Homfeld was right next to Fargis on the medal stand, having won the silver with "Abdullah." Together, Fargis and Homfeld led the U.S. Equestrian Team to the team gold that year in show jumping. Four years later, at the 1988 Summer Olympics in Seoul, South Korea, Fargis and a new horse, "Mill Pearl," were part of the American show jumping squad that won the team silver.

In 1992, Americans broke new equestrian ground by winning a team bronze in dressage at the Summer Games in Barcelona, Spain. It was the first medal of any kind in dressage for the United States. Four horses comprised that breakthrough team. One was "Graf George," a 10-year-old Hanoverian gelding out of Dee Muma's North Quarter Farm in Riverhead. Graf George was trained and ridden by Michael Poulin, who was able to hold onto the horse thanks to the financial support of Muma.

Muma sold Graf George in early 1994 to George Lindemann of Cellular Farms. In the meantime, she has gotten her hands on two new horses that show great promise in international dressage: "Wilder Kaiser" and "Kingdom Come." Could it be they who carry on the local Olympic connection?

A scenic sunset at Stephanie Powers' Five Tails Farm.

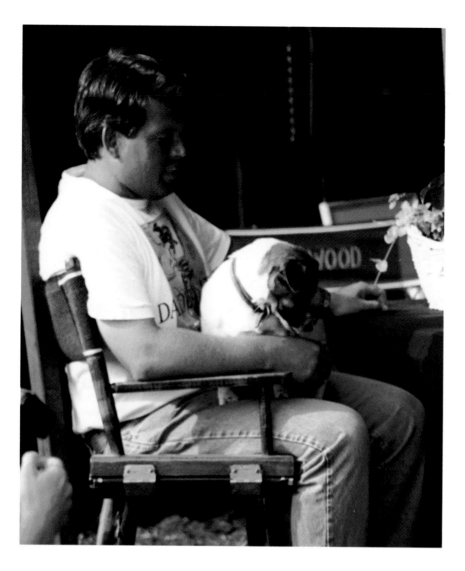

it will be fine. By the summer of 1980, our people were saying we want to win at the Hampton Classic."

By the advent of the 80's, Swan Creek and Topping Riding had established themselves as the top show barns of the Hamptons. They had riders competing on the national circuit, which was taking off in other parts of the country just as it had in Long Island. Mirroring the national trend, the Hampton Classic grew throughout the 1980's. The cycle, as far as local riding went, was repeating. Better shows begot better competition, which begot a greater demand for better training. America's success in the Olym-

pics, the prolific growth of the Classic made the sport popular. And so another big surge came to pass. In this round, the swing also gained momentum from economic boom times. Locally, a whole new wave of show barns rose up, SagPond being one of the more prominent.

Today, the Hamptons are rife with riding. Some of the best show horses can be found out here, and some of the best riders. Why? Simple. The shows. The Hamptons, like much of Long Island, now teem with quality shows that, to borrow a phrase from the political ring' have ridden in on the coattails of the Classic. In the summer - and even in the winter, with the recent addi-

tion of indoor rings - riders have shows from which to choose virtually every week. The choice includes local events like the Sagaponack Horse Show at Topping and the new South Fork series at Two Trees. On top of all that comes the Hampton Classic. With such a prodigious sum, it's no wonder riding has become so big in these parts.

"The Hamptons have become a great place to show," said Michael Meller, a trainer at Applewild Farm, which opened in 1993. "Basically, every weekend there is an A-rated show."

"What started very simple, very low key, very plain and unschooled has developed 25 years later into the horse being professional at what it does and we being professional at what we do," said Patsy Topping. "That level has evolved because of the horse shows we have."

"It's getting serious," added Patti Foster, the barn manager at SagPond. "The only way you can promote yourself is by showing at many places."

And so more and more each summer, local stables pack up the trailer and head out to the show rings. The scene has become very business oriented, indeed. Most farms have indoor rings that allow them to operate year-round.

Does this mean the old East End tradition of small backyard stables is gone, consumed entirely by the seemingly insatiable rise of show riding? No. Some stables remain low key, preferring to teach horse riding young people, without the stress of competition. Scuttlehole Farms is an example. There are even smaller operations, such as Hank Wintjen's place on Merchants Path in Bridgehampton.

"A little boy and a little girl can still have a nice backyard pony and keep it with one of the stables that doesn't go to shows and they can take care of it and have that wonderful bonding experience," said Patsy Topping. "There is an alternative. The alternatives are small, but they are there."

It's all there in Hamptons riding country. It's become big enough to be a landmark on the national show riding scene. Yet it still retains small pockets that recall where it all started.

Riding in the Hamptons has gone from small time to champion status. Above: *A rider collects a blue ribbon at the South Fork Classic, a new A-rated show on the East End presented at Two Trees Stables by trainer Bobby Ginsberg (opposite page).* Below: *A summer morning in Hamptons horse country.*

123

Sandron

Any overview of local riding in the Hamptons must begin with Sandron. It begins here not because Sandron is the biggest farm or the oldest farm or because it wins the most ribbons on Local Day. Sandron does not necessarily lay claim to any of those superlatives. But it does boast of two well-known names in show riding - not merely in the Hamptons, but in the world.

Joe Fargis and Conrad Homfeld, the operators of Sandron since 1985, have jointly amassed an armful of Olympic medals, World Championship medals, Pan-American Games medals, World Cup banners and Grand Prix titles, including one apiece at the Hampton Classic.

Joe Fargis and Conrad Homfeld at Sandron.

Editing the definitive highlight film is no easy task. But what is widely recognized as the shining moment came in 1984 at the Summer Olympics in Los Angeles. There, Fargis rode "Touch of Class" to the individual gold, while Homfeld guided "Abdullah" to the silver. Together, they shared the team gold with the rest of the U.S. Equestrian Team's show jumping squad.

Truly, in the Hamptons riding kingdom, Fargis and Homfeld are unofficial royalty. That's a distinction, though, they'd shy away from. Yes, Fargis remains a prominent fixture on the Grand Prix circuit. Yes, Homfeld has made a big name for himself both as a rider and as a course designer, which includes work in the Grand Prix

ring at the Hampton Classic. And, yes, both serve on the Classic's Board of Directors. But when it comes to day-to-day business, Fargis and Homfeld are very down to earth.

Sandron is low key as well. Tucked on 23 leased acres off Majors Path in Southampton, Sandron is open for only part of the year. It is open only to a select number of boarders. It is strictly private. There are no school horses on the farm. All horses belong to boarders, who train under Fargis and Homfeld.

For a good portion of the year, Fargis and Homfeld are not even at Sandron. They spend a lot of time on the road, training young jumpers and riding themselves. At the Classic, Sandron truly runs the gamut of compe-

tition. Some farm riders appear at Local Day. On Grand Prix Sunday, Fargis chases the big prize in the Crown Royal Grand Prix on a course designed by Homfeld. In the winter, the Sandron crew returns to its second home in West Palm Beach, Florida. There, Fargis and Homfeld and company ride and train at the Winter Equestrian Festival.

Fargis and Homfeld first came to Sandron from a farm they operated in Petersburg, Virginia. They were directed to the Majors Path property by Hampton Classic Chairwoman Agneta Currey, who boards her horses at Sandron.

The Majors Path property laid claim to a distinct chapter in Hampton riding history even be-

The view at Sandron, looking north.

fore Fargis and Homfeld arrived on the scene and renamed it Sandron (after a somewhat sandy farm they had run in North Carolina). The lot was a veritable Mesopotamia of Hamptons riding. In the 1920's and 1930's, it was home to the Southampton Riding and Hunt Club, which organized shows and hunts. At the same time, the club was the host of the Southampton Horse Show, the forerunner of the Hampton Classic.

The property saw varied use after those early golden years. At one point, the main farm building was used as a boarding house. (Room numbers are still visible over stable doors.) In the 1950's, the farm was home to a stable run by Diana Butler. In the latter years of that decade, the farm hosted the Southampton Horse Show for two years.

Fargis and Homfeld arrived in 1985 fresh from Olympic glory. They breathed new life into the old place, all the while keeping it a very limited operation. There are, only 18 stalls at Sandron. They are housed in wings that shoot off from the main barn. These L-shaped wings embrace a stone piazza that is highlighted by a fountain. As far as horse care goes, this open layout is pretty impractical. But it is unique - just like the two guys who run the place, two guys that rank highly on any equestrian list.

Homfeld readies a horse for competition.

Clearview

Southampton's Clearview on a clear morning.

Let's play a little word association. Name the first color that comes to mind when we say "clear view." Blue? How about this: Clearview? Easy: White, as in Bill White.

It's a gimmie. Clearview, the Southampton farm located on rolling terrain off North Main Street, has been in the White/Bishop family since the 1860's. Back then, White's maternal great-grandfather, James Bishop, established the farm. He raised cows, horses, vegetables. With the Atlantic blue visible in the

distance, he named the place Clearview.

The name has never changed. Only the operations have. After World War II, Bill's father converted Clearview into a potato farm. Bill, in turn, wrought a few changes of his own upon returning to Southampton in the 1980's, with wife Lin after a farming stint in upstate New York. With his daughters Morgan, Ashley and Brittan showing a big interest in horses, White turned Clearview into an equestrian farm.

In a way, the conversion brought Clearview out of a dark ages of sorts. For the necessity of potato storage, the barns were dark, with a subterranean feel. Just the opposite was needed for the new enterprise. So, with his knack for architectural design, White switched the old, dark potato barns into airy horse stables. This change over didn't exactly represent a break with the past. If anything, Clearview came full circle with its roots. Old foundations, windows and doors from the original horse and dairy barns were discovered

Clearview trainer John Lytle.

during the reconstruction. They were restored and recycled into the new buildings. From there, Clearview grew into the 32-stall operation it is today.

That Clearview would be given over to equestrian pursuits was only natural. The farm is situated in the heartland of Hamptons horse country. Joe Fargis and Conrad Homfeld operate Sandron just across the way. In the 1920's and 1930's, the land that now comprises Sandron, plus a portion of Clearview property, was leased by the Southampton Riding and Hunt Club.

Nowadays, about two-thirds of Clearview's 73 acres are devoted to equestrian uses as pasture, paddocks and trails. Deciduous shade trees are grown on the rest. As for the horse business, breeding comprises a large part of Clearview's operations. Half of the horses on the farm belong to Clearview, having been born and bred on the property.

Most are eventually sold. Some have a special place in the heart. "Clearview Classic" is one. A Golden Palomino born during the 1991 Hampton Classic, the horse is being groomed for a future appearance at the show.

As for riding, Clearview boards private horses and school horses and offers lessons. The farm has enlisted the services of trainer John Lytle, who signed on in 1994. Dressage specialists Jan Brons and Mary Ann McCaffrey, doing business as "Kilmore," came aboard in the same year. Mike and Carol Palmer handle the management.

While Clearview sports an impressive training staff, it is not a big show barn. Clearview makes few appearances at the events that saturate Long Island in the summer. Turned off by the "hurry up and wait" routine they found at various shows, Clearview riders opt to stay at home and practice.

"We don't see ourselves as a real show barn," said Bill White. "My original focus with the kids was, you can do four shows a year. Obviously, that went out the window. But the focus is on proficiency with the horse, advancing your skills."

"I prefer to stay at home and work with everybody," said Lytle, who, as trainer, stands to benefit most from regular show appearances. "Then, once they're ready, go to a show maybe once or twice a month."

The Hampton Classic, of course, is one exception to the Clearview rule. Every year the farm signs riders up for the show. They ride in a wide range of events, from Lead Line and Short Stirrup through children and adult jumpers. Look for the Clearview crew every year at the Classic; look for the Whites in blue.

Bill White and daughter Morgan.

Swan Creek

Patsy and Alvin Topping's family crest should read "Among the First." The Topping family is, after all, an American original, with roots tracing back to the 1600's. Patsy's family, the Clarkes, can trace theirs back nearly as far.

And when it comes to the horse business, the Topping place, Swan Creek Farms, ranks among the first professional stables in the Hamptons. Patsy and Alvin have been running their family-owned farm on Halsey Lane in Bridge-hampton since 1970. Prior to that, the 37-plus acres were potato fields farmed by the Clarkes. Once given over to horses, Swan Creek harvested ribbons instead of spuds.

In a way, the growth of the farm has mirrored the larger equestrian wave that has washed across the entire East End over the past 25 years. What started very simple and unschooled, Patsy maintains, has grown into an involved and highly professional industry. So it is at Swan Creek, which is one of the premier show barns on the East End.

There are 50 stalls in all at Swan Creek, 30 of which are filled by horses belonging to boarders. These boarders participate in a lesson and show riding program that runs year-round. There's no confusion as to when it's time to ride. In the summer, lessons are on Mondays, Tuesdays and Fridays. Wednesdays and weekends are devoted to show riding. Thursday is the lone day off.

The family Topping. This page: *Alvin oversees a lesson at the farm (top), while Patsy hits the show grounds at the Sagaponack Horse Show. (Patsy's sister Lolly Clarke is in the yellow shirt.)* Opposite page: *Jagger, Gretchen and Christian, the next generation.*

When winter comes, lessons run on the weekends in Swan Creek's indoor ring. When it comes to practice, Swan Creek riders go twice a day. Group lessons are held in the morning. Individual attention is provided in the afternoon as needed.

Patsy espouses group lessons as the ideal preparation for shows. She puts stock in individual lessons to pinpoint and correct faults. "We strongly believe in group lessons," Patsy said. "The reason for this is at a horse show you're not in the ring by yourself in the flat competition. So it behooves you to have group lessons to learn how to weave in and out of traffic and keep your focus with 20, 30 horses in the ring. But I also believe in individual lessons to focus on a problem and correct that problem. So we do a combination of both."

Lessons at Swan Creek cover Short Stirrup, Equitation and Hunter classes. Barbara Clarke, Patsy's sister-in-law, works with the adults. Patsy and Alvin teach the kids and take all riders to shows. Patsy also makes it a point to ride each student's horse to size up its habits, strengths and weaknesses.

With all the lessons, all the shows and all the riding, the Toppings like to limit the number of students to 30. There are only so many hours in the day and, if the number were any higher, much of the individual attention would get lost. Plus, Patsy says, "I don't like it to get any bigger because I just don't have the energy to do it."

While Swan Creek's lesson program focuses on private boarders, the farm has always

maintained a public front. It's a 10-week summer camp in which kids learn to ride using Swan Creek horses and equipment. The camp often serves as a starting point for Swan Creek riders who later get more involved in riding and showing.

The camp is currently run by Gretchen Topping and Alexandra Goldman. Gretchen, 18, is the second of Patsy and Alvin's three children. Jagger, 25, is the oldest; Christian, 13, the youngest. All are accomplished

riders. Jagger rides two horses, "Fanfare" and "Zelda," on the national show circuit. Christian's "Robin Hood" is a Grand Pony champ. Gretchen recently completed her junior riding career. She is a top Equitation rider who has shown at several prestigious events, including the National Horse Show. The younger Toppings head a long list of successful riders who have come out of Swan Creek, a farm that year after year wins big at the Classic. That's only natural. This farm is cut from quite an original cloth.

Topping Riding Club

There's a Sister Act playing at the Topping Riding Club. Whoopi Goldberg doesn't star. Anne and Emily Aspinall do.

Splashed across 40 acres of Sagaponack property owned by Bud and Tinka Topping, Topping Riding, the second oldest horse farm in the Hamptons, has been co-directed by the Aspinalls since 1978. Together, the two have become fixtures on the Hamptons equestrian scene. Both are long standing members of the Hampton Classic's Board of Directors.

Anne and Emily bring distinct talents to Topping. While Anne concentrates on training and teaching, Emily handles the business end. Does one have seniority over the other? It doesn't seem so. But, for the record, Anne arrived at the Topping farm first. It was 1970. Anne came out to work part-time for a college friend who was running the business at the time. Anne eventually left, only to return in 1974 to run the club full-time. Emily joined her four years later.

Anne and Emily own their business. They run it on land leased from the Toppings. At present, Topping Riding encompasses 37 permanent stalls, several riding rings and an indoor ring that makes the farm a year-round operation.

Topping Riding is a big show barn. In the summer, temporary stalls enable the Aspinalls to accommodate a clientele of approximately 50. Two trainers

Running Topping Riding Club can be a handful, especially when its time for the Sagaponack Horse Show. The club hosts the show twice a year. Top: *A reserve champ from the home show.* Bottom: *Anne Aspinall.*

Topping Riding, from the south side.

and 10 grooms are on hand to help run the show. That "show," incidentally, includes a collection of Labradors, who make themselves quite at home and attract other dogs from the neighborhood. Hence, Topping Riding at times looks part dog show, part horse farm. (Note the Lab X-ing sign as you drive in.)

Like other East End farms, Topping Riding is busiest in the summer. Club riders, most of whom come from New York City, are regular entrants on the Long Island summer circuit. Participation varies. Sometimes club riders appear in two or three shows a week. Sometimes they go more than a week between outings.

Of course, Topping Riding itself is a big part of the summer circuit. The farm's home event, the Sagaponack Horse Show, is one of the top dates on the local equestrian calendar. It is fitting that Topping Riding

hosts an important local show. The farm, after all, once staged the Southampton Horse Show, the forerunner of the modern day Hampton Classic.

Topping riders have always been regular showers at the Classic. (It could be argued that they were Classic riders before there even was a Classic.) Trained by Anne, club riders are schooled according to the Gordon Wright teaching method.

Named for Gordon Wright, a premier equestrian teacher under whom Anne studied, the method stresses the classical riding position and an exercise system to correct faults. The basic premise behind the position theory is that while the great ones will develop their own style, the average rider - and that means the majority - is best advised to follow the classical form.

As for correcting faults, the Gordon Wright method rec-

ommends an exercise, rather than practice, program. Anne uses boxing to illustrate the distinction. If a boxer is troubled by slow footwork, she says, the Gordon Wright method would put the fighter to work with a jump rope, rather than with increased sparring time.

In the show ring, Topping riders compete in a variety of classes, from short stirrup and ponies to children and adult hunters. Topping is primarily a hunter barn. Its riders do not compete in jumper events. Topping Riding competes on Local Day and during the week at the Classic.

Look for club riders in Short Stirrup, Children's Hunter, Adult Amateur Hunter, Amateur-Owner Hunter and Pony divisions. Look for club riders to be eager; look for club staffers to be a little harried. Jokes Emily, who carries a heavy work load as a Board member, "the Classic is what everyone looks forward to - at least the clientele, not necessarily the staff."

East End Stable

Andre de Leyer has been around horses so much for so long that you can't help but wonder if he doesn't have hooves in his boots instead of feet.

Truly, Andre de Leyer has horse in the blood. His father is the legendary Harry de Leyer, the Hall of Fame rider and trainer. Raised on his dad's farm, Andre grew up on horses, around horses, amid horses. Thus, it is no surprise that Andre has carried on the tradition, running East End Stables in East Hampton with his wife Christine. How much of a natural is Andre? Says Christine: "My husband was born and raised on a horse. He knows what he's doing. It's something that's been in his blood for a long, long time."

Andre and Christine have been at the helm of East End since the late 1980's. They took over from Harry, who had been operating as H & E Farm since relocating from Nissequogue. Upon their ascension, Andre and Christine renamed the farm East End. They recently bought the property outright and set to work on converting an old barn on the place into their home.

It would be fitting for Andre and Christine to live on their horse farm. It is their livelihood, their passion. Along with training, both ride competitively in hunter and jumper divisions. Both have been successful at the Hampton Classic. At the 1992 show, Christine placed fourth in the Sally Hansen Grand Prix. Two years later she won the Adult Amateur Jumper Classic.

Above: *The husband and wife team of Andre and Christine de Leyer.* Below: *Which way to the ring?*

Back at the ranch, the de Leyers, along with trainer Leigh Keyes, teach riding lessons to children and adults, from beginner to advanced. In the summer of '92, they established a summer camp for children. It's a camp that emphasizes horse care and stable maintenance as much as riding.

East End sports 40 stalls. Half are filled with horses belonging to boarders. Most of those riders commute out from Manhattan. The remaining stables are given over to horses bred by the de Leyers. Like most area stables, East End is a year-round operation. An indoor ring allows for winter riding, including several sanctioned shows. In the summer, East End tours the Long Island circuit, capping it with a yearly appearance at the Hampton Classic. East End rid-

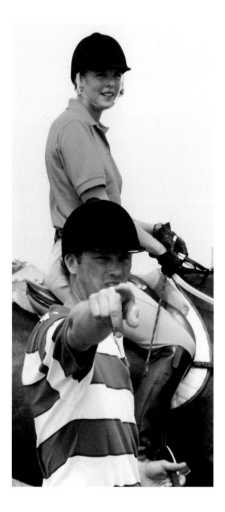

ers routinely show in Hunter, Jumper and Equitation divisions. Some of the younger riders are signed up for Short Stirrup. At the other end of the spectrum, Andre is a regular entrant in the Open Jumper division. Among the younger East End riders are Jennifer Gaines and Jamie McMahon, who routinely bring home ribbons.

While the de Leyers are big show riders, and while they hail from checkered horseman stock, they insist on an unpretentious, low-key atmosphere at East End. "This is a casual, down-to-earth farm," says Christine. "You don't feel you have to put on boots and breeches to ride here. You don't have to keep up with the Joneses."

But how about keeping up with Big Daddy? Harry, the patriarch, is a Hall of Famer. He is famous for his "Dutch" horses. He is famous for rescuing a horse bound for the glue factory - for a mere $80 at that - and turning him into a Grand Prix champ. He even once held a record for the highest jump. How do you follow in those footsteps? "You don't," says Andre. In his case, he just goes about the business he loves. That alone has satisfied both son and father.

"I never worry about filling his footsteps," Andre said. "I like to do it to please him, sometimes. It makes him feel good when I do good. I love the business and I'd do it anyway. It makes him feel good that his son is still carrying on the family tradition."

"As far as the pressure, there is none," Andre added. "I

Top: *Andre de Leyer, horseman.* Bottom: *The mare Cinnamon and the foal Star, a recent arrival at East End.*

hope someday to maybe get where he's gotten. But times have changed. The horses are on a different caliber than where they were 20 years ago, even 15 years ago. The courses that they jump are real technical, the jumps are much higher. He (Harry) once set a record at six feet, nine inches.

The record now is seven feet, nine and a half inches. It just keeps climbing."

Will the name de Leyer climb higher on the equestrian ladder? In Andre and Christine it continues to endure. That seems to be of greater value.

Hillcrest Stables

Debbie Wilcox has been running horse farms for more than half her life. That would make her an old hand at the business, right?

Yes and no. By the time Wilcox hits 35, she will have logged 20 years in riding. Since 1975, when she opened Four Seasons Farm in Westhampton at the age of 15, Wilcox has worked her craft with horses. Now, two decades later, the youthful Wilcox is the hand of experience that guides Hillcrest Stables, a family-owned farm on Middle Road in Riverhead.

The 30-stable farm sits on property owned by Debbie's parents, Catherine and David Wilcox. It is run by Debbie, her sister Darlene and brother Dean. Anita Morely and Lee Santos serve as assistant trainers. Before it was Hillcrest, the Wilcox property was home to a duck farm. When that industry collapsed in the late 80's, Debbie moved her horse business over from Westhampton, the same 10-stable operation she had run as a teenager.

Was Wilcox too young when she started? In a way, yes. Until Wilcox got her driver's license, she couldn't take Four Seasons riders to shows. But Wilcox has always had an innate knack for her business. She realized that when she travelled extensively to Europe in her late 20's. Burned out by the business back home, Wilcox's equestrian fire was rekindled by the discipline of dres-

Debbie Wilcox, stable operator since the age of 15.

sage. It also confirmed that what she had been doing was right all along. "The whole experience in Europe just opened up doors," Wilcox relates. "I had so much new information to work with. It was like starting all over again."

Not surprisingly, dressage is the basic staple at Hillcrest. All riders who take lessons there are schooled in the art. About a third of the riders compete in that discipline. The remaining riders move on to show riding.

All the kids horses at Hillcrest.

Hillcrest has a strong junior riding program that has been showing at local shows and at the Hampton Classic since, well, since Wilcox could legally drive.

Currently, there are some 60 riders who train at the Riverhead farm. These riders go year-round thanks to Hillcrest's indoor ring. Summer, though, is the busy time. Twice a week the farm packs up and heads to recognized shows across Long Island. Hillcrest riders compete in hunter and equitation. Tiffany Cornacchio of Baiting Hollow, Lauren Barth of Aquebogue and Gretchen Goodale are among the Hillcrest riders to watch.

Amid regular training, Hillcrest complements its program with clinics that feature outside pros. Hillcrest also offers a service that enables riders to lease horses rather than buy them. Another benefit from her tour of Europe, Wilcox says, was learning how to fit a rider with an ideal mount.

Speaking of which, Wilcox seems to have found an ideal horse for herself in "Schatzi," a Dutch warmblood. With Schatzi, Wilcox is aiming to make the U.S. Equestrian Team in dressage within the next few years. Clearly, it is the art of dressage that drives Wilcox.

While dressage incorporates the fundamentals, she says, it lays the groundwork for unlimited advancement.

"The leading trainers recognize the importance of dressage in all disciplines," she said. "We find it really changed the overall picture of the rider and how they jump the horse. You see the balance. It's much more fluent and accurate. That's what dressage is all about: Creating harmony between horse and rider. It's a never-ending process. If you're really willing to develop style and technique, you can always improve."

Two Trees Stables

David and Jane Walentas are relative newcomers to the East End equestrian scene. But it's no secret they've made up for lost time.

When the husband and wife team bought the old Carwytham Farm on Hayground Road in Water Mill from the Baldwin family in the spring of 1993, they wasted little time launching an ambitious series of projects. Through renovations, restorations, additions - and a name change - they succeeded in making Two Trees one of the largest horse farms in the Hamptons.

What's been done? Here's the laundry list. In their first year the Walentases added new paddocks, and built a new barn. They re-did the existing barn, adding a lounge, locker room and tack room on the second floor. They renovated the existing indoor ring and set to work on building a new one; they renovated existing homes on the property for use as staff housing. They carried out site improvements, such as moving electrical wires underground and upgrading the septic system. And last, but far from least, David and Jane, after some initial resistance from Southampton planning officials, built two polo fields. "We've done a lot in one year," remarked Jane. "And we're just getting started."

Say what you want, the Walentases are newcomers with zeal. And they're unique in another way. Unlike other horse farm owners or operators in the Hamptons, David and Jane do not come from much of an equestrian background. This was apparent in the way in which they came upon the old Carwytham place. What drew them wasn't the horse farm, but the pure beauty of the land. "It wasn't as if we were looking for a horse farm," Jane said. "We really bought the property because we thought it was beautiful property."

The Walentases, however, recognized the established equestrian tradition and amplified it without missing a beat. They renamed the place Two Trees in honor of David's New York City real estate firm, which, ironically, was named for a partner's South Carolina horse farm. ("It's kind of fitting that it's come full circle," David noted.) They brought in a handful of trainers, and quickly established a lesson program.

Two Trees riders travelled to shows in that first summer, including the Hampton Classic. The farm even hosted a few events, which included South Fork I and II.

For David, buying the farm was a jump back to boyhood days. "I grew up on a farm when I was a kid - a dairy farm in upstate New York," he said. "I lived on a farm with a pump and an outhouse. We've always loved farms and animals. We saw this land and we loved it. It's really going to be a serious, full-service farm."

It already is. Two Trees sprawls across 130 scenic, softly rolling acres along Hayground Road. All 130 acres are given over to equestrian pursuits. There will be nearly 90 stalls once the new barn is complete. The two indoor rings will be unique. No other East End farm has more than one. The existing ring at Two Trees measures 12,000 square feet. The new one will be twice as big. Then, of course, there are the polo fields, as Two

Two Trees owners David and Jane Walentas.

Trees strives to cater to polo players as well as show riders.

As for the show riding, Two Trees is a regular on the Long Island summer circuit, with riders competing in Adult Hunter and Jumper, Junior Hunt and Jumper and all

children's events. The farm picks its spots carefully, but usually shows at least once a week. Several circuit events are hosted by the farm. That included four in the summer of '94. It's a tradition the Walentases hope to continue.

SagPond Farm

At SagPond Farm you don't have to worry much about running out of riding room. There are only, oh, some 150 acres upon which to roam. And at SagPond Farm you don't have to worry much about finding a free paddock. You've got just about every ring imaginable to choose from, including a Grand Prix course with all the jumps.

No, you won't lack for much at SagPond. Owned by wine entrepreneur Christian Wolffer, SagPond is one of the biggest stables in the Hamptons. In fact, a quick glance shows that in terms of pure dimension, only Two Trees is in the same class. Vast and scenic, SagPond spreads across 150 Sagaponack acres nestled between Narrow Lane and Montauk Highway. The Wolffer home sits on the property. So does the farm's other prime operation, the grapes of SagPond Vineyards.

As far as the equestrian element goes, SagPond became a private stable in the 1980's. Gradually, the farm opened up to lessons and boarding. Sag-Pond now boasts of 30 farm horses. They are the backbone of the farm's extensive lesson program, which is taught by a large training staff that features open jumper Ray Texel. Trainers Scott Kemery, John Wittenborn, Eva Weiner, Doreen Johnston, Kelly Carll and Deanne Dominguez were also aboard in 1994. Along with the private lessons, SagPond hosts a summer pony camp. And, with the addition of

The riding options seem endless at SagPond Farm, which stretches over 150 acres in Sagaponack.

a state-of-the-art indoor ring in early 1992, SagPond can stay busy in the winter with lessons and sanctioned shows.

SagPond likes to bill itself as the most complete indoor and outdoor riding stable on the East End. It's not an idle boast. The new indoor ring is housed in the main barn. The Grand Prix ring sits on the outskirts of the property. It has all the jumps, banks and ditches you can jump a horse at. Then there's the grass hunting field, the sand jumping ring, the Fibar ring, the dressage ring.

The overall stall count is 50. The woodwork in the stables shines. The atmosphere is bright and spacious thanks to skylights in each stall. The stalls even come equipped with heat lamps. Elsewhere, a new barn is being built to accommodate 16 horses that belong to the Wolffers.

It was all a costly proposition, no doubt, but it's paid off. The care shows in the horses. The clientele have come in droves. "It has come on faster than expected," said Patti Foster, who serves as barn manager while colleague Dai Dayton works as farm manager. "It's always been good in the summer - it's a summer place. Now, our year-round business has just about doubled in the past two years. We have plenty of room to ride. The horses love it here. It's like a country club."

SagPond riders range in age from four to 60. They show regularly on the Long Island circuit, as well as at larger shows in Virginia, Connecticut and upstate New York. And, of course, SagPond shows at the Classic. Farm riders compete both on Local Day and during the week. You can find them in most classes: Short Stirrup, Equitation, Hunter, Open Jumper. In all, some two dozen riders go in under the SagPond banner. Along with them go the seven trainers, 14 grooms. It's a large contingent. It has to be. It represents one of the Hamptons largest farms.

Stony Hill Stables

The story of Stony Hill Stables is a simple one: Like mother, like daughter. At the 10-plus acre farm off Town Lane in Amagansett, Elizabeth "Wickety" Hotchkiss has carried on where her mom, Liz, left off after 35 years. The lesson programs, the array of summer camps remain much the same at the stable that is the oldest running horse farm in the Hamptons.

The basic philosophy also remains the same. At Stony Hill, you'll learn to ride a horse and you'll learn how to take care of it. Good care of it. See that clock on the wall in the office? It says "Time to Muck." It's no lie. At Stony Hill, you're going to get some dirt under your nails. There's no handing off horses to a groom.

"Our whole thing is our concern with the quality of riding and the whole learning process," said Wickety. "Where the other barns cater to wealthy people, the people who come here really want to get involved in the whole sport. They want to get involved in taking care of their horse. That's very important. I hope it always stays like that."

Wickety learned her brand of horse business from her mother. Liz Hotchkiss opened Stony Hill in 1954. Some of her early students included Patsy Clarke, who would open up a stable of her own 16 years later with husband Alvin Topping. That stable, Swan Creek, would become one of the most prominent horse farms in the Hamptons. So it's clear to see to what extent Hotchkiss was a founding mother of East End riding.

Hotchkiss ran Stony Hill until 1989, when she headed out to Missouri to start a new farm. Wickety picked up the reins back at Stony Hill. It was a natural succession. Wickety had grown up on the farm. Undoubtedly, it's where she picked up her nickname, the origin of which remains a stable secret. "It's not being disclosed," Wickety maintained. "You won't guess in a million years. No one has yet."

Wickety: What's in a name? Maybe something to do with her slimness? No. Croquet? No. Fragile bones? No, again. And no one else is telling - not Caryn Lowe, the stable manager, not Kristine Snellenberg, the

lessons. "We put a lot of flatwork, which is dressage, into our jumping," said Wickety, "because what jumping essentially is, is flatwork with a few jumps thrown in."

Stony Hill shows regularly on the Long Island summer circuit. The stable shows in preparation for the big one: the Classic. Stony Hill never misses, regularly signing up riders in Short Stirrup, Children's Hunter and Equitation, including Medal and Maclay. There's no way Stony Hill would miss out. "Every spring parents come: We want our children to go to the Hampton Classic," Wickety reports.

Ah yes, behind every kid stands a parent hoping to be made proud. At Stony Hill, where daughter takes after mother, it appears to have come to pass.

trainer, and probably not even Lynn Smiley, the assistant manager, who wasn't around on visiting day.

Along with keeping their secret, all these young ladies help Wickety run Stony Hill's 30-stable operation. With an indoor ring, Stony Hill is a year-round operation. Lessons are also offered in the fall and spring, as well as in summer.

Like other Hampton stables, summer is the busy time at Stony Hill. For one, the farm offers a bevy of camps. There is a pony camp, a Short Stirrup camp, a horse camp, even a horse show camp for advanced riders. Camps like these have long been a staple at Stony Hill Stables. "We were the originator of the pony camp many, many years ago," Wickety stated. "Now everyone has a pony camp."

Stony Hill is big in Hunter, Equitation and Dressage training. Dressage is Wickety's department. A devout dressage rider, it's the skill she teaches to all Stony Hill riders. Snellenberg and Lowe handle the jumping

Scuttlehole Farms/Meadow View

Partners in Time. **Top:** *Mary Bailey.* **Bottom:** *Junellen Tiska and one of Scuttlehole's young riders.*

Scuttlehole Farms could be called "Horses R' Us." The place just brings out the kid in you.

Operated by Mary Bailey and Junellen Tiska, Scuttlehole is a stable located on the 60-acre Meadow View farm on Seven Ponds Towd Road in Water Mill, owned by Barnes & Noble. It's a storybook land for child riders. It's a place of lesson programs, and of pony camps. And, befitting a farm tucked amid quiet woods, it is a place to learn about horses without the pressure of constant show riding.

"The purpose from the start was to get kids to be comfortable around the animals and to develop skills - a sense of confidence, responsibility," said Bailey. "We wanted to offer an alternative to riding just for the purpose of showing."

Not surprisingly, the Scuttlehole farm is a reflection of its operators. It is a combination of kid sense, as it were, and horse sense. Bailey provides the latter. Despite growing up in Brooklyn, she comes from a horse background. When she came out to the East End to attend nursing school, Bailey said, she insisted on staying at a place with horses. She got her wish when she signed on with Liz Hotchkiss at Stony Hill Stables.

Bailey finished school and went into nursing. It was her job for 22 years. Still, she managed

to put in time at Stony Hill, then at Carwytham. Then she met Tiska, a teacher at the Hampton Day School. They took stock of their respective skills. Together, they figured, they could run a horse farm for children. Tiska and Bailey found land to lease, a property formerly used to breed thoroughbreds. Stables, a barn were already on the grounds. In March of 1991, the two partners opened up shop. While there are adult riders at Scuttlehole, the farm was geared toward kids from the get-go. The idea was to teach children not only how to ride, but how to care for a horse. Bailey said she borrowed that strategy from her mentor, Liz Hotchkiss

Bailey and Tiska did maintain the old dimension of the previous farm. They continue to breed thoroughbreds. But they also effected changes. They added some stables (there are 16 in all) and added a pony ring. In time, Scuttlehole became home to a chapter of the East End Pony Club. In the spring of '94, Scuttlehole gained some prestige by hosting a regional equestrian final of the Special Olympics.

Scuttlehole has indeed grown. So, too, have its riders. Many of them have been at Scuttlehole since the start. They arrived as beginners. As they grew, they advanced in ability. Starting in Short Stirrup, they have progressed to Equitation and Hunter classes. Kelly Bailey, one of Mary's two children, competes in Adult Amateur Hunter. In the meantime, a younger wave of students has washed through, refilling the shoes in Leadline and Short Stirrup.

It's true Scuttlehole isn't a big show barn. ("I like to be competitive, but sometimes you can be too competitive," Mary said.) But there is one constant: The Hampton Classic. Scuttlehole has shown there since opening in 1991. Bailey maintains the Classic is a show without peer. As she says, it's a show where the kids can ride with the pros. In a way, it's sort of the cherry on top after a summer of hard work in the sun. For Bailey, there is much to savor in the work itself. "I'm very happy doing this. This is what I love to do." Loving your work: Now that's kid's stuff.

Applewild Farm

Applewild Farm may be the new kid on the Hamptons horse block, but the kid is already wise. Applewild, owned and operated by the husband and wife team of Larry and Wendy Schmid, was established in the summer of 1993. It is part of the housing lot the Schmids purchased off Meadow Court in Bridgehampton.

Yes, it's small - only 15 stalls - but it's homey. The Schmids, independent trainer Michael Meller and most of the riders at the farm are all in the 30-something age group. Most came in with plenty of previous experience in the show ring. They know what it's like to be high in the point hunt for indoor circuit qualification, and the same goes for their horses. It's an experience that belies Applewild's status as the New Kid. "Most of the horses that come here are show horses, very competitive show horses," said Meller.

In the Schmid household, Wendy is the experienced horse hand. Larry, a non-rider, handles the farm duties. He's at home on his John Deere tractor. Wendy, a lifelong rider, is at home in the stable. After working and riding at local farms, Wendy revels in running her own place. "I'm in heaven," she said. "It's really great. I don't know anybody who's had the opportunity I've had. I'm very, very lucky."

Applewild sits on 16 acres tucked between Meadow Court to the east and the junction of Scuttlehole and Mitchell roads

to the west. It is laid over old potato fields that have been developed into a small neighborhood. Larry speculated that Applewild could embody the wave of the future: the conversion of old farms into more active uses that still maintain an agricultural flavor.

Applewild still bears a distinct rural touch, bordered as it is by lush cornfields. Apple trees stand out front. Larry planted them upon naming the place Applewild after a farm run by his great-grandfather in Fitchburg, Mass.

The Schmid farm is entirely private, open only to boarders. The current group trains in Hunter, Equitation and Jumper classes. "We're not a riding academy," noted Larry. "You can't come off the street and take les-

Top: Larry and Wendy Scmid. Bottom: trainer Michael Meller

Applewild is named for a farm Larry Schmid's great-grandfather owned in Fitchburg, Mass.

sons. We have our boarders, and our boarders pretty much do what they want. We built a pretty decent farm. We're small, but we're a very pretty place."

And a tight one, too. Because of the proximity in age, because of the small number, the Applewild gang enjoys a distinct degree of esprit de corps. "At this barn we're all young," Wendy said. "We're all on the same level. We all take it seriously, but we all want to have a lot of fun. We have a lot camaraderie. That gets lost at a lot of the bigger barns."

Little or not, Applewild makes the rounds on the summer circuit and does well. With their prior experience, most Applewild riders came in with the Hampton Classic already on their resumēs. The 1994 show, however, marked their first appearance at the Classic under

the red and black colors of Applewild. Riders Michael Bassett, Kimberly Flotz and Laura Traphagen joined Meller and Schmid in Applewild's inaugural run. All competed in various Hunter divisions. Traphagen tried her hand in Adult Jumper. There wasn't much trepidation among these new Applewild riders. The kids have been there before.

Chapter VI: The Players

The Riders

Each year, more than 1,000 riders, more than 1,000 horses appear in the spotlight at the Hampton Classic. At an event watched by celebrities and actors, it is the riders and the horses who are the true stars. The saddle and the rein are their props; the show ring their silent, solitary stage.

Show riding is unique as a sport in that it is a blend of two living components. A horse is often no better than its rider, and a rider no better than his or her horse. One cannot win without the other. The Classic, through its history, has seen famous pairs: Olympic stars Joe Fargis and Mill Pearl; Hall of Famers Rodney Jenkins and Idle Dice.

Show riding is also unique in its sexual equality. Whether male or female, riders and horses compete on equal footing in the same ring, over the same course. Like other shows, the Classic has seen male and female winners - both among riders and horses. Rider Beezie Patton won the 1993 Classic Grand Prix. She was the fifth woman to do so. The year before, Jeffrey Welles guided the mare "Serengeti" to the winner's circle.

As for prestige, show riding ranks with yachting, golf and tennis as a so-called elitist, big-money sport. Then again, given the salaries baseball, basketball and football players command, what sport isn't? Show riding, though, may have the others beat. Its roots are aristocratic and it fairly drips with cash.

Grand Prix rider Tim Grubb.

You've got to pay to play. While a backyard horse can be picked up for a couple hundred bucks, the typical show mount goes for five figures. Top-line horses, particularly jumpers, go for six. On top of that must be added yearly care and stabling costs. A quality stall can take on the dimension of a modest mortgage.

That's just at home. Many farms take their act on the road, riding the circuit for much of the year. Travel and show costs add up. All told, the American Horse Shows Association estimates the average rider kicks out anywhere between $20,000-30,000 in equestrian-related expenses a year.

They can afford it. AHSA numbers show that 40 percent of all families involved in show riding take in annual incomes in excess of $150,000. The average value of their residences: $425,000.

The ethnic composite of show riding? Predominantly WASP-ish, upper class and upper middle class. There are few minority riders.

All of this is the stereotype, of course. And while there is a grain of truth in every stereotype, it is also true that the world of riding, like any population, is very diverse. There are different ages, different skill levels. That's another unique characteristic of show riding. At a given event, all talent levels are on display. So it is at the Classic, which runs from Leadline to a $100,000 Grand Prix.

Show riding has its pro riders, it has its aspiring juniors. It has children and teenagers trying to balance school and riding; it has working adults raging on the weekend. It has its rich kids, yes, but it has its regular folks, too - working class people who somehow manage to scrape by and play along.

They're all at the Classic, and once they don their riding cap and breeches, they may be hard to tell apart. The following is a sampler of some of the faces behind the numbers.

Joe Fargis

You could say Joe Fargis has had a storybook life when it comes to show riding. He's gone from a kid painting fence rails a la Tom Sawyer to a top show jumper who has attained glory around the world. Fargis has starred in the Olympics, in World Cups, in Nation's Cups, in Pan-Am Games. He's done it in the United States, in Europe, even in Korea. But the one show with which the name Joe Fargis is truly synonymous is the Hampton Classic.

Perhaps that's because Fargis has much more to do with the show than just riding. Yes, he rides every year. He even won the Grand Prix in 1991. But there's more to it than that. He's a member of the Board of Directors. As a trainer and a rider, he kicks more entry fees into the Classic coffers than all others, according to show manager Steve Stephens. Fargis even comes out on Local Day to judge the Leadline contest. It's not just some appearance in which the big star goes through the motions. He talks to each little rider, giving camera-clutching parents plenty of time to capture the moment.

All these elements tie Fargis tightly to the Classic. But there's a stronger bond. Fargis, as the operator of Sandron Farm in Southampton, is the show's local hero. Fargis came to Southampton with his partner Conrad Homfeld in 1985. It was one year after the two had won the individual gold and silver to lead the U.S. Equestrian Team to gold at the 1984 Olympics.

Joe Fargis takes a ribbon at the Classic.

Fargis had indeed risen far up the equestrian ladder, especially for someone born in Brooklyn, far from horses. Fargis didn't get his first look at a horse until his family relocated to Vienna, Virginia when he was seven. One day he went to a friend's house after school. The friend's mother ran a horse farm. Little Joe was quickly hooked. "I loved the horses," Fargis recalled. "I took off and rode and rode - to the exclusion of everything else."

Fargis was a quick learner. Was he a natural? "Well, I'm not going to say I was the best rider there ever was, but I sure enjoyed riding. You can learn a lot up to a certain point. Then, at the top, I think there's a natural knack that comes into play. I would say I've developed a natural feel for horses and riding and jumping."

Before all that, Fargis developed a feel for the paint brush. He cannot recollect his first horse show. But he does remember the circumstances that allowed him to ride back in those early days. He was not an indulged prodigy. He had to earn his keep. "The lady's name was Mrs. Dillon - she was the proprietor of the riding school. And once a year we had a big show. Mrs. Dillon had these white fences at the farm. I remember painting white fences. The reward was to ride in the show." With Tom Sawyer pluck, Fargis advanced as a rider. And, as he got better, he developed a basic philosophy. "I try to consider the horse first, period," Fargis said. "He's the one doing all the work. At all costs, you have to consider the horse first."

Jeffrey Welles

Nothing beats a Grand Prix that is won as the day's last ride, and that is exactly what Jeffrey Welles did at the Hampton Classic in the summer of 1994. Welles, only moments removed from a fall, hopped aboard the young thoroughbred Irish and rode a clean, high-flying round in a winning 49.2 seconds. In doing so, Welles stole the day from Michael Matz, who was on the verge of winning his third Hampton Classic Grand Prix. Matz occupied not only first, but second place, prior to Welles' dramatic ride.

For Welles, the 1994 coup was his second championship at the Hampton Classic. He won his first in 1992 with Serengeti. Ironically, it was Serengeti that tossed Welles hard onto the rails of an obstacle during the 1994 jumpoff. Physically shaken up, Welles had to regroup to ride Irish. There wasn't much time. That worked to his favor. "There wasn't a lot of time to think about not going

out there," Welles would later say. "If I had time to think about it, it probably wouldn't have turned out this way."

Welles knew he had a winner in Irish. The horse had won a bronze medal at the 1992 Olympics in Barcelona under Norman Dello Joio. Irish worked best when pushed to a gallop, and that's what Welles needed. He had been with the horse for just a few months. But in crunch time, they were a perfect meld. Irish seemed to float over jumps. When he and Welles crested the final obstacle and bolted for home, the Grand Prix crowd erupted. Fans had been treated to the show jumping equivalent of a game-winning home run with two outs in the bottom of the ninth.

The Grand Prix win was the first for the Welles-Irish tandem. Welles had won previous Grand Prix with Serengeti, Zoef, Silver Spirit and Czar. With Webster, he was part of the gold medal team at the 1989 Na-

tional Horse Show and Washington International Horse Show. Welles, born in North Carolina in 1962, has been riding since the age of six. As a junior, he trained at Ronnie Mutch's Nimrod Farm. He currently resides in Newtown, Ct.

At 22, Fargis was a member of the U.S. Equestrian Team that won the Nation's Cup in Switzerland in 1970's. Other successes followed: a Pan-American Games championship in 1975; a spate of Nations' Cup titles; Olympic medals in 1984 and 1988. In 1984, he became only the second American to win an individual Olympic equestrian gold. He rode Touch of Class cleanly over 90 of 91 obstacles, an Olympic record. In 1988, he took the silver with Mill Pearl, the horse with whom he had been named Leading International Rider the year before.

Amid all of this, what has been the defining moment? "It has to be the gold medal that everyone knows about," he said. "There are many things that pro-

vided a lot of satisfaction, like winning at the Hampton Classic."

The Classic. After all, although Fargis had won around the world, the one prize he had yet to capture resided in his own backyard. All that changed in 1991. Only several months removed from a fall that had broken his arm, Fargis guided Mill Pearl to the Classic Grand Prix title. They were later named the Grand Prix League's Eastern Conference horse and rider of the year.

Another bad fall, one in which he suffered a compound leg fracture, kept Fargis out of competition for much of 1992. He returned strong the following summer to win the Grand

Prix at Lake Placid.

He continues to ride and train year-round. He reportedly takes on any rider at any time. Walk the Classic grounds one day. You're bound to hear a story about how Fargis, just several days removed from the Olympics, came out to someone's backyard farm.

It seems a stretch, but you can't help but think it's true. He's a backyard guy who's got gold medals and a stained white paint brush in his riding treasury, and he doesn't plan on stopping soon. "I never gotten to that point seriously," he says. "I have no problem with my life. I enjoy it on a day-to-day basis."

Rodney Jenkins

Rodney Jenkins has the distinction of being the winningest Grand Prix rider at the Hampton Classic. That's hardly a surprise. Jenkins is the winningest rider at plenty of other shows, too. In fact, Jenkins is the all-time winningest rider in all of American show jumping.

As of the summer of 1994, Jenkins was the owner of 70 Grand Prix titles. Three of them came at the Hampton Classic. He won in 1981 with Idle Dice, in 1983 with Coastline and the following year with Sugar Ray. Of the three, and of all the champion horses Jenkins has ridden, Idle Dice is the most famous. The horse was a charter member of the Show Jumping Hall of Fame. With Jenkins in the saddle, Idle Dice brought home more than $400,000 in Grand Prix winnings.

For his career, Jenkins has already surpassed the million mark. After winning his 70th Grand Prix in 1989 in Palm Beach, Jenkins stepped away from show jumping to train racehorses. The retirement was not permanent. In 1994, at age 50, Jenkins returned to the show ring. With his trademark red locks still intact, Jenkins rode in from his Montpelier, Va. farm with Equador and the aptly titled S & L Second Honeymoon, the horse he rode in the Grand Prix.

Jenkins appeared at the Classic that summer and went gunning for a fourth Grand Prix win. To the delight of the crowd, he advanced to the jump off aboard Second Honeymoon. In the end, he came up short on a day won on the last ride by Jeffrey Welles.

Michael Matz

Michael Matz will always be a fan favorite at the Hampton Classic. And he will also always be a favorite of at least two other people out in the world, even if they know nothing of show riding.

Matz is remembered at the Classic for winning two Grand Prix. The first, amazingly, came in 1989 less than two weeks after he survived the crash of United Airlines Flight 232 in Sioux City, Iowa. The tragedy killed more than 100 passengers. Matz was credited with saving the lives of two young children. He received national recognition. ABC-TV named him "Man of the Week." If Matz seemed super-human at the time, he heightened the perception by winning the 1989 Hampton Classic Grand Prix with Schnapps just ten days after the crash. He returned in 1990 to win a second straight Grand Prix, this time with Heisman.

Riding clean has been the name of the game for Matz. The Pennsylvanian's riding career dates back to the early 70's He is second only to Rodney Jenkins in career Grand Prix wins. He has also won the U.S. Equestrian Team championship five times. He has twice ridden in the Olympics; he has won gold medals in the World Championships and Pan-American Games.

In 1994, Matz was on the verge of winning a third Hampton Classic before Jeffrey Welles stole victory away on the last ride. But by finishing both second and third with The General and Olisco, he actually won more money. Some people are golden.

Michael Endicott

Michael Endicott is proof of the Hampton Classic's drawing power. A Californian from just outside San Diego, Endicott came to the Classic in 1986 and won big as a junior. The next step up was the Grand Prix level, and Endicott pledged to himself he'd return East only when he was ready to ride with the best.

The best meant riding at the Hampton Classic. In 1994, Endicott made his return and proved his mettle by reaching the Grand Prix jump-off. "Basically, I vowed I wouldn't come back till I could compete with these people," Endicott said. "Now I feel I'm there. I've got the horses, I've got the education and I've got enough clients and investors to support the trip."

Endicott is something of a whiz kid, California style. He is recognizable for his sunglasses, which he wears even while riding. He is one of the few riders to do so. Born in 1968, Endicott made his name known fairly quickly. In 1985 he was the Rolex Junior Rider of the Year. The following year he won the national junior jumper championship, a feat that was fueled by success at the 1986 Hampton Classic.

This was big stuff, and Endicott was still only 18. By 1987 he was competing on the Grand Prix level among riders old enough (some of them) to be his parents. As a Grand Prix jumper, Endicott developed close to home, riding on the Western circuit. He attended Marymount College, graduated in 1990 and

started Pegasus Show Stables. Out West, Endicott enjoyed success with Mon Bambi, a French-bred gelding. He later acquired several Dutch breeds (Zadok, Maybe Forever), a Hanoverian (Bound For Glory) and an Irish-bred (U-Two). He also picked up Grand Star, and it was with that horse that Endicott reached the 1994 Hampton Classic Grand Prix jump-off.

Endicott has got a lot of riding ahead of him, and he intends to ride to the end. "Riding a horse, for me, is something that gets in your blood when you're young," Endicott said. "Once it's in your blood you can never let it go. For me it's a lifelong thing. I don't think I'll ever get out of it alive. I'm sure I'll retire or die still involved with horses."

Family Affair: Team Leone

"All in the Family" could be the name of the Leone story, except that there's no Archie. There's no Meathead either, just good horses. The Leones are three brothers from New Jersey - Armand, Peter and Mark - who all compete as Grand Prix riders. Sponsored by Crown Royal, their moniker is "Team Leone," and each brother brings a reputable list of credentials to the club.

Armand, the oldest by three years, has represented the U.S. Equestrian Team in two Nations' Cup competitions. In 1988, he was a five-time Grand Prix champ. Peter, the middle brother, has also represented the U.S. Equestrian Team, both at world championships and as a second alternate for the 1988 Olympics. Mark, the youngest, emerged on the Grand Prix level after a successful junior career. He was an AHSA Medal champ and the 1982 USET Young Rider of the Year.

Above: *Peter Leone and daughter at the Grand Prix ceremony.* Below: *Mark Leone.*

While the sport has claimed the affection of all three brothers, the Leones, strangely enough, do not come from a show riding background. Their father, Armand Sr., doesn't ride. He's a doctor. So is their mother, Rita. She didn't really discover horses until she and Armand moved to New Jersey from New York City.

Rita did light the spark that drew the boys to riding. They started with ponies and, in order of age, progressed up the ladder. It was like going from Little League to high school to the bigs, except with horses. "We weren't in it for the winning, we were in it for the participation and the family," Mark Leone recalled. "It would be like a family outing for us. It just kind of stayed with us all. The horses really keep a common bond between us. The riding keeps us in close contact."

Nowadays, Armand Jr. doesn't ride as regularly as he once did. He is both a doctor and a lawyer working in New York City. That has left the riding to Peter and Mark. Both ride the Grand Prix circuit; both run farms. Peter operates Lion Share Farm in Stamford, Ct. Mark is at home with Ri-Arm Farm in Franklin Lakes, NJ. By the way, there is a little word play at work with Ri-Arm Farm. "Ri" is for Rita, "Arm" for Armand. And, in case you didn't notice, Peter Leone is the Grand Prix rider who traditionally brings his son or daughter along when it's time to ride in the ribbon ceremony. With the Leones riding is simply a family ritual.

Family Affair: Team Falco

American Horse Shows Association statistics show that 40 percent of all show riding families earn in excess of $150,000 a year. Numbers like that feed the perception that, for many, show riding is a mere out-of-pocket expense.

While that may be true for some, it's not the case for everyone. It's certainly not the case for the Falco family of Bay Shore. The Falcos, Vincent and Mary and three kids, are one of those modest-income families that scrapes a little, pinches a little so that one of the members can have a little extra. In this case, the Falcos pinch for their youngest daughter, Marcella, who is a Medal and Maclay Equitation rider. Marcella has been riding since age three. She enjoys it and, during her ten years of show riding, she's been successful. For that reason, the family has supported her, from small ponies through medium ponies through large ponies to, finally, a horse by the name of Vision Quest.

The horse is kept in a backyard barn. Still, there are lessons and show costs that put a strain on the Falco budget. But they manage, and throughout the year Marcella competes at local shows across Long Island and in Connecticut. At the end of each summer the entire family and some friends make the trip out to the Classic. They set up quarters in several trailers and stay the week on the show grounds.

"We struggle all year to

The extended Falco family of Bay Shore, L.I.

get here," Vincent Falco said one night at the Classic while cooking up steaks on a grill outside the family trailer. "I'm self-employed. It's hard when money comes in to put some aside for lessons at the end of the week. You have to work a couple of hours extra at the end of the day to make up for it."

"You do it for your kids, you don't do it for yourself," added Wendy Falco. "We give up a lot. The parents do. The kids do, too. Marcella used to run track. But she can't do after-school things any more. Her whole time is devoted to this."

Marcella's introduction to riding came via a flier in the mail advertising summer recreational programs. That's pretty unique.

What isn't so unique are the financial circumstances surrounding the girl's riding. Other riders, says Wendy Falco, are in the same position. "We don't have the big bucks, but you find a lot of people like us doing this," she said. "They give up other things so their kids can do this."

Why? "Insanity," Wendy chuckles. "You start small and before you know it you're at the Hampton Classic."

The ones who manage to swing it wind up at the Classic. There are others not so fortunate. "It's an expensive sport," Wendy said. "If it was less expensive more people could enjoy it. There are a lot of kids out there with talent whose parents can't do anything about it."

Joan Lunden: Weekend Warrior

Joan Lunden is best known as the host of ABC's "Good Morning America." But she is known in another light by people who, like her, balance a career with riding.

Lunden, despite her big name, is the prototypical Weekend Warrior. You know the kind. They work the weekdays, play hard on the weekends. But show riding is a bit trickier. The sport entails more than just hopping on a horse every Saturday and taking a spin around the ring. Practice is critical, and that means warriors like Lunden have to make room in a busy weekday schedule for riding lessons. "You can't compete unless you're going to ride regularly during the week," Lunden attests.

For any working person, this is easier said than done. In Lunden's case, it's even more of a stretch. Hers is a job entailing travel, interviews, studio time. Plus, her work is based in New York. Benchmark, the farm at which she rides, is in Connecticut.

"It's tough to know how I can carve out time for my riding, my workout, my work and my kids," Lunden said. "I schedule my life to the point of the neurotic, but it's the only way I get in all that I want to get in. For me, going to a lesson is just as important as an interview. I know if you don't ride for a couple of weeks you really lose it."

Lunden has been around horses for much of her life. As a girl growing up in California, she learned to ride bareback. It was pure Western style - barrel racing, trail rides. She wasn't exposed to English-style riding until she came East and signed her daughter up for lessons. It didn't take long for Joan to give it a try as well. "As I sat watching her riding and jumping I wondered, 'why am I not doing this?'" Lunden recalled. "One day I took lessons, the next year I had eight horses."

Mother and daughter were both hooked, though the horse count has since been cut in half. Joan's daughter, Jamie Krauss, has emerged as a top children's rider. Joan plies her craft in Adult Amateur Hunter and Equitation. Together, Joan and Jamie show throughout the year, travelling to a show each weekend. Hundreds of other riders run the same schedule, and Joan likes to point out that they traverse common ground. The same faces are seen week after week, bonds steadily form.

"It's an interesting sport in that it's not one horse against another horse," Lunden said. "Everybody rides together and goes against a standard of excellence. Consequently, among the people you compete with there's a wonderful feeling of camaraderie."

In hopes of protecting other riders, as well as her own privacy, Lunden rode under an assumed name when she first starting showing. She wasn't sure if her identity would unduly influence a judge, and she didn't want other riders to suffer for it. Lunden changed her thinking,

though, at the behest of Kip Rosenthal, her trainer. Lunden, Rosenthal reasoned, should be proud of her accomplishments and thus should go by her real name.

Rosenthal had to work more psychology with Lunden following a bad fall in 1992. Lunden's shoulder was broken. The injury kept her off a horse for a year. But even when she returned to the saddle, her confidence was still badly shaken. That's when Kip stepped in. "When I got back on I was very fearful," Lunden said. "Kip took me back and made me comfortable with the basics of riding."

Lunden returned to the show ring just four weeks before the 1994 Classic. She had been absent for two years. "Now that I'm back riding I'm doing good in my schooling lessons," Lunden said. "I have to get back in the ring. I have to go to show after show." That's the spirit of the Weekend Warrior.

Anna Elias: Earning Keep

There is a certain stereotype of the child rider. It is of the well-off kid who shows up for private lessons nattily dressed, jumps on a prepared horse, completes the riding, then hands the horse off to a groom.

Sure, it happens. But there is another type of young rider, and that's the kid who is involved in all facets of the sport, both the riding and the maintenance. One of those young riders is Anna Elias. The business of horse care has always been part of the deal for Elias. Perhaps it's because she came to riding relatively late - at 17, she was competing in her first and last year as a junior. Or maybe it's just the way Anna is.

An Equitation rider and Jumper, Anna rides with Somerset Farm in East Norwich, N.Y., her hometown. For much of her childhood, though, Anna lived in Queens. She always wanted to have a horse, but living in Queens made it out of the question. The situation finally changed when her family moved into the more spacious suburbs of Nassau County.

That's when Mum's the Word arrived. "Anna had to do this," said her mother, Ruth Elias. "It's like breathing and sleeping for Anna to have a horse."

It's also like a business. Her parents got her Mum's the Word under the condition that she take care of it. Anna had no problem with those terms. In fact, she welcomed them. "I'd rather take care of her than have someone else take care of her," Elias

Grooming her own horse is part of the deal for rider Anna Elias.

said while applying a poultice and wrap after a day of showing at the Classic. "This way I know she's taken care of correctly. She also knows me better. I'm not just her rider. She's been my best friend for the past year because I go everywhere with her."

There were limits on that.

In the fall of '94 Anna headed up to Northampton, Massachusetts to attend Smith College. The summer had been productive, though. Elias aimed to qualify for the national finals in equitation and did so in the Maclay class.

Rowlanda Blue Stephanos: Rising Star

Teenager Rowlanda Blue Stephanos has garnered success at each stage of her young show riding career. Her aspirations? The Olympics.

If a name like Rowlanda Blue Stephanos doesn't destine you to stardom, what does? Maybe, when it comes to show riding, good consistent work in the ring.

Though only 14 years old heading into the 1994 Hampton Classic, Rowlanda Blue already had a starry list of accomplishments to match her Hollywood-esque name. In 1993, Stephanos so dominated the Children's Hunter division that Power & Speed, the official publication of the National Grand Prix League, identified her as one of the top five riders in that class in the East Region.

Stephanos, a Sagaponack resident who was training at Two Trees Stables in 1994, has emerged as a top rider in a relatively short span of time. She has done so steadily, progressing step by step. It started at the age of seven at the Thomas School of Horsemanship in Melville. Rowlanda signed up at the suggestion of her mom, Pamela, who had ridden at Thomas as a child. Rowlanda quickly took to riding. She did well at small local shows, eventually graduating into her first horse. Purchased by her step-father, Barry Allardice, the first mount was a pony called "All That Glitters."

Contrary to the saying, "All That Glitters" was gold. In their first year together, Rowlanda and "All That Glitters" did so well in large pony competition they qualified for the Washington International Horse Show. Stephanos was just 12 at the time.

This match seemed destined for further greatness until nature intervened. In a dramatic growth spurt, Rowlanda shot up six inches, much of it in her legs (by 14, she would stand 5'11'). Thus, after one glorious year, Rowlanda had outgrown her prize pony.

Rowlanda's family continued to be supportive, however. In a way, the new family created through the marriage of Pamela and Barry was bonding through Rowlanda's riding. Why break up a good thing? Allardice found Rowlanda two new horses, "Sailaway" and "Seconds at Last." With horses and family in tow, Rowlanda hit the circuit in Florida. "We used Rowly's riding to start a whole new family, and we got hooked on it," mused Pamela.

With her new horses, Rowlanda initially tried moving up a few notches from Large Pony Hunter. Bypassing the next step, Children's Hunter, she entered Large Junior Hunter. It proved to be too large a leap, literally. The higher jumps - 3'6" rather than 3'0" - were daunting. As a result, she opted to go with Children's Hunter.

It was a wise move. It was the natural progression and Rowlanda excelled. Training with Patrick Rice and Laura Bowery in Brookville, Rowlanda racked up the ribbons. The 1993 Classic was the crown jewel of the summer. With "Seconds at Last," Rowlanda swept all classes to win the Children's Hunter Championship in her section. With "Sailaway," she captured a reserve championship. Rowlanda went on to win the $2,500 Children's Hunter Classic. In the final tally,

Margaret Stark: Balancing the Books

As with other riders who attend public schools, Stark's absences for shows dates aren't exactly understood.

If there's one thing child riders quickly learn, it is this: School and riding don't exactly mix, especially in the public sector.

Margaret Stark of Huntington, L.I. is well versed in that lesson. While moving through the show riding ranks as a teenager, Stark has managed to stay just above board at Huntington High School - not in terms of grades (she does do well), but in attendance. "My school has an attendance policy and I just make it each year," Stark said while competing in Children's Hunter Horse at the Hampton Classic the summer before her senior year. "The teachers want to kill me," she added while patting a pretty gray named Blue Ridge. "All for these guys."

Stark confronts a quandary faced by many riders who attend public school. While attendance rules are often bent for athletes in traditional sports, show riding is seen in an entirely different light. In fact, it doesn't seem to be seen at all. Convincing school officials that one must miss class in order to ride a horse is no easy task, according to Stark. "People in my school get out for basketball games and county championships," Stark reported. "I get marked for an absence."

So Stark must plug away, often arising before dawn to crank out homework. The teenager shows year-round with Fletcher Farm. In the summer, Stark and other Fletcher riders hit the shows two or three times a week. In the winter, they usually show every weekend at local events.

Stark has been riding since she was a little girl. She became interested while attending a dog show. What caught her eye that day weren't the dogs, but the horses at a neighboring farm. She came back for lessons and has stuck with

it since. And, like many other child riders, Stark has learned to balance show rings with school books. Heading into her senior year, Stark suspected the juggling would get even trickier. Her trainers, who had recently bought a new farm, were hoping to build an indoor ring. They were also ready to turn it up a notch on the riding circuit. A winter trip to Florida was in the forecast.

More riding will mean more missed school, which means more effort just to keep up. But Stark has done it. She has to. Anything below a "B" and she'll have to stop showing. "I have to, or I can't keep riding," Stark said. "I have to get up and do my homework at four o'clock in the morning. It's hard, but it's worth it."

she was awarded the Miller's/ Marshall & Sterling Grand Hunter Championship, which incorporated all sections at the Classic. This showing qualified Rowlanda for the Zone 2 Hunter finals in Harrisburg, Pa. There, she was reserve champ.

After the accomplishments of '93, Rowlanda was ready to move up to Large Junior Hunter in '94. This would be a year of change. There was the new division, for starters. There was also a new home and a new school. With Rowlanda riding so well, the family decided to move out to horse country, leaving Manhasset for Sagaponack. This brought her to the Hampton Day School, which was more cooperative and understanding than the public school in Manhasset when it came to a student who periodically missed class to tour on the horse circuit.

The move also brought a new trainer and stable: Bobby Ginsberg and Two Trees in Bridgehampton. With Ginsberg, Rowlanda hit the Florida circuit in the spring. She lived the travelling horse life with Ginsberg and his fiancee, Jennifer Mannino. They lived in a cramped trailer for months. In the mornings, Rowlanda attended an on-site school for child riders. In the afternoon, she rode. In the end, she and "Seconds at Last" finished third for the overall circuit.

Back on Long Island, Rowlanda continued training with Ginsberg. Along with the Hunter discipline, she took on Equitation. A division more challenging than Hunters, Equitation

introduced Rowlanda to changing courses and higher jumps. The new class brought on a new horse, "Go West." So far, horse and rider have done well. According to Ginsberg, Rowlanda has made the strides she has due to a combination of skill and willingness to learn. "There's a lot of natural talent," the trainer said. "For someone her age, she's really won a lot. There are actually a lot of kids who are envious of her. When she showed in Children's Hunter they said, "oh no, Rowly's back."

At the 1994 Classic, Rowlanda was a ubiquitous presence. She competed in Large Junior Hunter with "Sailaway" and "Seconds at Last" and in Equitation with "Go West." Where to ultimately? Said Rowlanda, "I want to try to go all the way to the Olympics." "Aim high, right?" asked mom. "Yes," said Rowlanda Blue.

With that name, who could miss? Rowlanda Blue

Rowlanda trained with Bobby Ginsberg at Two Trees Stables.

Stephanos: So unique, so catchy and so perfect for horse riding with its smooth gallop of syllables. Where did it come from? Rowlanda: That's from Roland, her grandfather. Blue: That's the nickname of her dad, who never cared much for his name George. What's in a name? A little chapter in a story larger and still unfolding.

The Hampton Classic routinely draws riders from all over the United States. The state-by-state list includes not only states on the East circuit, but from the Midwest and West as well.

In 1994, 25 states and the District of Columbia were represented. There were also riders from St. Croix, St. John and Bermuda. Riders came in from Canada (Grand Prix rider Mac Cone) and from Venezuela. (Junior/AO jumper Alberto Carmona). Grand Prix riders Tim Grubb and Yolanda Garcia, though American citizens, hail from England and Spain, respectively.

As for the stateside picture, New York fields the most Classic riders, usually about two-thirds of the total crowd. No surprise there, given Local Day. New Jersey and Pennsylvania are usually tops among the rest of the country.

Led by Connecticut, New England ranks highly, too. In 1994, every New England state was represented at the Classic save Maine.

All in all, virtually the entire East is accounted for. Basically, you could take the Classic exhibitors index in one hand and a map in the other and, starting from Long Island, move south down the Atlantic Coast without missing a state. Jersey, Delaware, Maryland, Virginia, the Carolinas, Georgia and Florida have all had riders at the Classic in the 90's

Riders have come from the deep South: Esther Kane of Houston and Mara Winston of New Orleans were up for the '94 show. Riders have also come from the Midwest. There have been Buckeyes from Ohio and Hawkeyes from Iowa. In 1994, Hayley Vaughn came out from Des Moines. The same year, Laura Grand-Jean made the trip from Barrington, Ill. Emily Watson travelled in from Leawood, Kansas.

Don't overlook the Left Coast. Led by Grand Prix rider Michael Endicott, the field from California alone numbered more than a dozen in 1994. Washington (Allison Evans) and Oregon (Amy Kinlan) were also represented that summer.

There were 25 states in all - half the country with a piece of one showground.

Jersey Farms: Two for One

In a business steeped in competition, two farms from New Jersey take a unique tag-team approach to show riding. Windham Hill Farm and Hilltop Farm, two stables out of northwest New Jersey, appear at shows like the Hampton Classic together. They hit the road together. They share the same stables and tack room at the show grounds.

They don't just do this occasionally. They do it all the time. They are, in essence, one entity comprised of two separate bodies, a sort of yin-yang in the horse world.

This arrangement is the product of the relationship between the trainers at the respective farms. Michael Dowling trains at Windham Hill. Bethi Dayton trains at Hilltop. Dowling says the two share the same philosophy when it comes to riding. Both, he says, are goal-oriented. Each year, the farms set targets for their riders, the best of whom ride on the national circuit.

The similarities between Dowling and Dayton only go so far. Ironically, the differences are what really nurture the twin-farm approach. Dayton is a stay-at-home trainer, while Dowling likes to roam. "We click," Dowling says. "There are a lot of people in the industry you can do this with, but it's rare to have a working partnership."

Thus, Dowling heads up the entourage when show time beckons. Dayton, however, isn't a total home-body. She appears at the Hampton Classic, the show that both farms count as their favorite. Nothing better, they say, than a summer trip to the Hamptons. And in the land of the group rental, why not double up?

Michael Dowling, trainer at Windham Hill in northwest New Jersey, teams up with Bethi Dayton and neighboring Hilltop when it comes time to hit the circuit.

What's in a Name?

As any pet owner can attest, the naming of an animal is no task to be taken lightly. Time, thought, creativity must go into the process. When it comes to all that, horses are no different from dogs and cats. The names of horses that have appeared at the Hampton Classic make that apparent. There has been a Leapy Lad, there has been a Touch of Class. Both, fittingly, were Grand Prix champions.

Horses often have two names: one a flowery name for the show ring, the other a simpler tag for around the barn. The show names, naturally, are the more creative of the two, and the range of reference points is remarkably wide. In 1994, there was everything from magazines (Gentleman's Quarterly) to baseball teams (Cincinnati Red). There was even a Red Sox, whose rider, Kate Rice of Sherborn, Mass., evidently had no fear that the jinx that haunts that team would carry over to her horse.

Many horses were named for places - incongruously, at best. Chestnut Ridge, N.J., was home to Athens. Likewise, Kalifornia came from New Canaan, Ct. Nothing seemed to fit. Valhalla rode in from Long Valley, N.J. Rodney Jenkins

brought Ecuador up from Virginia. Grand Canyon went home to Rhode Island. Chesapeake took harbor in Buffalo. And, if you'd like to see Disney Land, the horse, you'll have to go to Tim Grubb's place in Somerville, N.J.

Do you like rock and roll? Many riders apparently do. There were horses named for bands (The Who, Steely Dan) and for songs (Good Golly Miss Molly, Stormy Monday, Mississippi Queen, Chantilly Lace). A few bands were more popular than others. Who do you like better, the Beatles (Twist n' Shout, Let It Be) or the Stones (Jumpin' Jack Flash, Ruby Tuesday)? It was a toss up, apparently, with the Classic crowd.

Maybe you like things a little more funky. The group War got air time with Low Rider and Cisco Kid. Or perhaps you prefer Reggae, Rhythm & Blues, Melody, Happy Rhythm or Fascinatin' Rhythm. They were all there. So was the Hillcrest Music Man. For those of a classical bent, there was Beethoven, Mozart and the Nutcracker Suite.

There were many readers at the Classic. Some went in for the heavier stuff (Beowolf, Ulysses and Finnegan). Lord Byron was in attendance. So was Shakespeare, along

with characters Juliet and Calaban. Robin Hood was a particular favorite. Maid Marian, Friar Tuck and the title character were on hand. So were Heidi, Captain Hook, King Arthur, Billy Budd and Gulliver.

Fans got a read on Great Expectations and A Separate Peace. Miss Marple was in the ring, trying to cypher a jump or two. Let's not forget the Good Book. Goliath and Noah's Ark were both floating about.

Maybe all that reading called for a drink. You had Absolut, Bud Light, Southern Comfort, Gin, J.D., Chilled Rum, Michelob, Harvest Wine and two Sambuccas to choose from. Who would supply? Bootlegger or The Rum Runner. Both may have led you to Whiskey Before Breakfast.

Some names were more topical than others. Could the 1990's have been better represented than by Virtual Reality? The placement of other names in the Exhibitor's Index was uncanny. Good as Gold, Tough as Gold and Silver Dollar, all separately owned, were listed in consecutive order. Pocus Hocus followed Midnight Illusion: Was it mere coincidence?

Ours is a TV age, so it should be no surprise Macgyver, I Spy, Vision Quest, Who's the Boss, Mr. Rogers, Tales from the Darkside and Batman all saw air time - in the ring, that is. A Double Feature played. It was Eraser Head and Tootsie.

The name game goes on. Jack Trainor's horse was Bittersweet, June Kaneti's a Perfect Gentleman. Cyndi Edwardson had the Man of the Hour. Madeline Lewis had Such a Deal. There was a Blind Date, a Flirtation. Brenna Watson had Probable Cause.

The horses of Laurie Jakubauskas were not to be messed with. One was Locked and Loaded, the other Armed and Dangerous. And Dana Lefkowitz? Her horse was Just Right.

A Second Chance, with Panache

It wasn't looking good for Panache. The promising two-year-old racehorse had just broken a leg and the owner wanted the horse put down. But thanks to an adamant veterinarian, Panache survived and healed. And, thanks to an adamant rider, Panache was reborn as a show jumper.

Nowadays, Panache is a Preliminary Jumper ridden by Diana De Rosa, the Press Officer of the Hampton Classic. Through persistence and some top-flight training, De Rosa has guided Panache into a legitimate jumper. She thanks Dr. Robert Fritz for having the horse around in the first place. A track veterinarian at Belmont Park, Fritz insisted, against the wishes of Panache's owner, to keep the horse alive after he broke his leg in a freak accident.

Fritz had been impressed with Panache upon first seeing him stride into Belmont. "This was a horse, a thoroughbred, that was one of the prettiest, most beautiful two year olds I had seen at Belmont Park," he said. "When a nice horse comes in the front door, he catches your eye."

This was the mid 1980s. Panache, purchased as a yearling at an auction, spent a year being broken in at a farm in Maryland. Then, as a two year old, he came north for further training at Belmont. Panache progressed nicely and started racing. He placed fourth at Saratoga. Back at Belmont that fall, he started winning by larger and larger margins. A glittering career appeared to be dawning. "He looked like he had all the promise in the world," Fritz said. "We thought we had a real legitimate Derby horse on our hands. The trainers got high on him, so did the owner. And he just filled out and looked even more magnificent."

Then came the accident. While tied up for grooming one day, Panache broke free of his chain. The groom had temporarily stepped away. Panache, unchecked, took off full tilt down the barn. At the end, he turned sharply to the left.

That's when the bone broke. It was a Condylar fracture of the right foreleg cannon bone. Fritz sadly made the diagnosis and called the owner, who wasn't interested in saving the horse.

He told Fritz to put Panache down. Fritz balked. Sleep on it, he told the owner. But one day, even a second, did not bring a change of mind. Fritz wouldn't budge either. Finally, the owner gave in. He said, "Bobby, if you like the horse so much, you can have him," Fritz recounted. "I was just interested in saving the horse. I figured he'd make a nice horse for someone down the road."

The road, as it turned out, led right to Fritz's home in Huntington. After performing a two-hour operation in which he inserted two titanium screws to hold the broken bone in place, Fritz took Panache home. There, the horse mended.

Now, when Panache was given to Fritz, the horse's full jockey association certificate was not made part of the deal. That meant Panache would be unable to perform again as a racehorse. That was OK. Fritz's friend, Lucille Passione, had other ideas for Panache. She saw him as a show jumper.

Panache, however, didn't care much for the new discipline. He was a big, strong and obstinate horse, one difficult to handle. Frustrated, Passione was close to giving up on him. Then she thought of De Rosa, a friend and neighbor. That was the day De Rosa came home to find Passione and Panache waiting in her driveway. As De Rosa tells it, she stepped out of her car, into the ring and onto a new partner. "I knew instantly this horse was special," De Rosa said.

Panache wasn't exactly putty in De Rosa's hands. He could still be difficult. Refusals were frequent. Occasionally, De Rosa was thrown. But the rider hung tough, and as she and Panache rode on a chemistry developed between the two.

Perhaps it was fated. Horse and rider, after all, were both rehabilitation projects. Panache had his broken leg mended by Fritz; De Rosa had been born with a congenital dislocated hip socket that was surgically repaired when she was a child. It was, you could say, a perfect match of imperfection.

De Rosa and Passione continued to train Panache, with De Rosa doing all the riding. They eventually started showing, first in Adult Amateur Jumper, then in Preliminary. In the process, a three-way partnership developed. Passione, who owned a 50-50 share in Panache with Fritz, handled the grooming. The horse showed under her name. De Rosa, did all the riding. Fritz the vet was happy to drive the van.

While De Rosa has worked with renowned horseman Joe Fargis, she remains the only rider to jump Panache. Supporters hope horse and rider will continue to climb the show jumping ladder together. The prospective is that both have the potential. In combination, they seem to be one of those teams that exceeds the sum of its parts. "Joe said Panache has a lot of trust in me, and I have a lot of trust in him," said De Rosa. "There are times when he's about to stop and I'm not and he just keeps going. I think he really tries to do his best for me. It seems he doesn't give up if I don't give up."

If Panache is no quitter it may be because there were those who did not quit on him: a vet, a trainer, a rider. It was their constancy that ensured this horse would ride again.

By Design: Conrad Homfeld

When fans take in the action in the Grand Prix at the Hampton Classic, they are admiring the handiwork of Conrad Homfeld no matter what the horse, no matter who the rider. His professional touch is on display every round. But don't look for him in the Exhibitors Index. His name's not there. Instead, his signature is on every jump, and every obstacle in the ring.

Homfeld has been designing the Grand Prix course at the Hampton Classic since the mid-1980's The oxers, the verticals, the water obstacles: Nothing is out there in arbitrary fashion. They are placed and decorated as Homfeld decides.

As a rider and a trainer Homfeld wants his courses to be challenging to horse and rider. Ability, courage, obedience in the mount, and horsemanship in the rider must be tested. Homfeld also takes aesthetics into consideration. The course must be appealing to the eye, both for riders and spectators.

Perhaps above all, Homfeld is guided by this philosophy: A course should reflect the roots, the history of equestrian sport. Those roots, he asserts, are mostly of a rural bent. They run in the fox hunt, in military endeavors - places where riders were confronted with natural obstacles, such as stone

walls, streams and hedges, gates and fences. Homfeld says he strives to reflect those elements in his courses, whether it be in the standards, the plantings and decorations or in the jumps themselves. "I like to have it grounded in something from the past," Homfeld related. "Jumpers evolved from a fox hunting background and the cavalry. That's our roots. Now, a jump with a Calvin Klein sign - well, that's progress. But still, I think a course that loses touch with the past looks alien. It doesn't represent where we come from."

Riders have taken note of Homfeld's handiwork. "This Grand Prix field is probably one of the nicest in the country," said rider Michael Endicott of California. "It's got atmosphere, it's got natural obstacles."

Course design is just one facet of Homfeld's interest in show jumping. His riding career was highlighted by World Cup titles in 1980 and 1985, an individual silver medal and team gold at the 1984 Olympics. He posted the same medal combination at the 1986 World Championships. Oh yes, he also won the Hampton Classic Grand Prix in 1982.

Nowadays, Homfeld spends a lot of his time training riders with Fargis, both at Sandron and at their winter home in Florida. They spend a good part of the year on the road, training and appearing in shows. Summer brings Homfeld and Fargis to the Hamptons, and to the Classic. While Fargis continues to ride at the show, Homfeld occupies himself with setting up the course. It's a week-long chore. The course is altered after each event. At the close of each day, it is overhauled.

Homfeld says he's been interested in course design since his early 20's. The appeal? Not so much creativity, he says, but control. In a sport in which much is beyond control - a rider, say, may be having a good day, while his horse is not - course construction allows the designer to put, well, a jumping world in his hands. "I don't know if I consider myself creative," Homfeld said. "As a rider, there's so much you can't control. It's a nice change in this business to do something you can control so much of."

Homfeld gives the waterwheel jump a lookover before the start of the Grand Prix qualifier.

By nature, the world a course designer creates is calculated and ordered. Riders are expected to treat each obstacle in a certain way. But that's not a given, and it's that unpredictability that gives Homfeld as much a reward as the control factor. "It's not an exact science," he says. "There's always an element of surprise to it. It doesn't always work out the way you planned."

Grand Prix courses feature various types of obstacles. There are verticals, which are jumps composed of a single plane - perhaps a stack of rails or a wall. Verticals are usually the highest jumps on the course.

Another main staple is the oxer. An oxer is a single jump comprised of two or more vertical planes. Where verticals present a problem of height, oxers present problems of height and width. Horses must go up and across. Oxers can be square, which means the front and back are of uniform height from stack to stack, or they can be of varying height, which provides a ramp effect, going from low in the front to high in the back. Square oxers are considered the more difficult of the two.

Looking around the course, you will no doubt spot a water obstacle or two. All legitimate outdoor Grand Prix rings have them. In some cases the water may be a secondary element of a jump, perhaps a ditch at the bottom of a vertical. This water isn't window dressing. It can affect the way a horse handles a jump. Water can be the obstacle itself. These obstacles, known as open water jumps, are flat, broad pools that must be cleared by the horse. Not only that, but the horse must also clear a strip of tape on the landing side. Touching either the water or tape nets four faults.

While open water obstacles may seem easier to clear than five-foot verticals, they are deceptively difficult. Without rails, they provide no bearing, no lift, no target for the horse to shoot for. Open water jumps at the Classic range from 12 to 14 feet across. The maximum distance of 16 feet is reserved for the Olympics.

Any of the above obstacles can be lumped into a "combination." Combinations are a series of jumps, usually two or three, that comprise a single obstacle. The jumps come in rapid succession, with only one or two strides in between. (This contrasts with a "line," in which the obstacles come individually and are separated by at least three strides.) Because combinations are considered a single obstacle, a rider must clear its jumps in order. If one jump is missed, the rider must start at the top.

There are other types of obstacles that may be seen at the Classic. There are bank jumps, which, as the name implies, require a rider to jump while going either up or down an embankment.

A variation on that is the Pulverman's Grab. This jump has a sunken road look. Riders move down a bank, clear a jump at the bottom, then move up and out. This is the only jump not featured at the Classic.

Whatever the course, riders and horses must make their round without benefit of a trial run. The only preparation al-

At Homfeld's direction, jumps at the Classic are given a natural touch.

lowed is known as walking the course. That's what riders can be seen doing before show time. Decked in their colorful jackets and black riding caps, riders are counting the strides between jumps. (Typically, 12 or 14 feet computes to one canter stride of a horse.) Walking the course enables riders to determine the ideal place to jump and, at the Classic at least, figure out the best way to solve Conrad's design.

Chapter VII: Behind the Scenes II

Life on the Lot

There is whole a life to the horse show world that exists beyond the spotlight of the show ring. In fact, it could be said that what happens in the ring is but a fragment of the total horse show picture - a tidy, close-cropped and picturesque detail from a panorama dominated by darkened stables, dusty practice rings and travel-worn trailers.

The picture abounds with characters. There are the typical people you would associate with horses: trainers, grooms, vets, blacksmiths. But there are also food vendors, suppliers, merchants, photographers, launderers and, at places of extended stay, schools.

Indeed, show riding is not only an industry, it is a travelling, almost self-contained community. The mobile town rides along the yearly circuit. Here in the East it opens in Florida in January and ambles northward through summer before the indoors in the fall. Many of the farms that ride the circuit are on the road the whole time, without a glimpse of home until Thanksgiving. But those who do it say it's not that torturous. "It's really not that bad," confessed Jeannie Somers, a groom with Marley Goodman's Turtle Lane Farm in Palm Beach. "We do have time off in between shows."

For one week in late August/early September the mobile town goes up in Bridgehampton at the Hampton Classic. The stabling tents house the

The corner of Stable and Main. The show riding circuit is a veritable travelling community that moves from town to town.

principal citizens, the horses. As for the riders and their entourage, lodgings are typically taken in nearby hotels. At the Classic, house rentals are a big ticket, it being the Hamptons, the great land of the summer rental. Others stay right on the show grounds. Some grooms, and some smaller farms that need to watch the wallet will establish quarters in trailers right on the lot. Most are cramped, but many are well equipped. Running water is provided. The other necessities of life? Food concession-

A Day in the Lot Life. **Top:** *Hay is unloaded, water is gathered the day before the show opens.* **Above:** *Katey Grau and Clothes Line Laundry Service handled the wash load at the '94 Classic.* **Right:** *Vincent Falco gets ready to cook up a few steaks on the back lot after a day at the show. Falco and his family were among those who stayed on the Classic grounds during the week.*

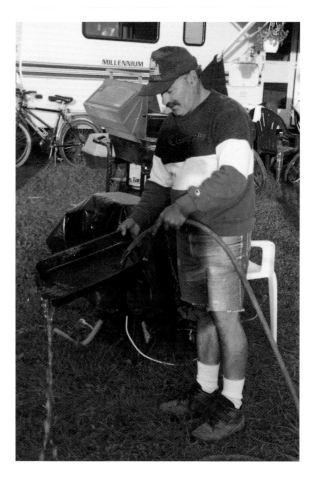

aires travel along with the troops. So do many shopkeepers who, during the week, set up in the Boutique Garden. These merchants provide goods to a ready-made clientele: boots, tack, riding garb, horseshoes. There is even a monogramming service, which travelling stables use to identify their equipment and clothing. Why? So it doesn't get misplaced - in the laundromat, for instance.

Incongruous as it may seem at first, a mobile laundromat can be found on virtually every A-rated show ground. On second thought, of course, it seems perfectly natural. There's a lot of work and competition going on at a horse show. A lot of clothes get dirty - both people clothes and horse clothes - and who's got time to track down the local laundry service? "We travel so much it's hard to find a laundromat, and no one has enough energy when they get off at six," said Katey Grau of Clothes Line Laundry Service, which set up shop at the Classic in a trailer located at the back of the show lot. "We pulled in on Monday and there were, I don't know, a thousand barns waiting it seemed."

A typical show week for travelling barns begins a day or two before the show. The crew drives in, unloads the horses, prepares the stables, acquires feed. At the Classic, exhibitors purchase feed from Agway, which is located just across Snake Hollow Road. And what exactly were Classic horses dining on? Basically either Timothy hay or alfalfa hay. Of the two, Timothy hay was the popular choice. Al-

falfa hay is greener and richer. If horses aren't used to it, Alfalfa hay can be a little too, well, moving, and people who travel the show circuit are already doing enough moving - and cleaning - for that.

The trainers, the grooms, the vets and all the other characters who labor behind the scenes in the horse world come the Classic's way but once a year. The following is a look at their lives.

The Trainers

There are three main players, as far as the competition goes, at every horse show: riders, horses, trainers. For every horse and rider that takes to the ring, you can bet there's a trainer looking on critically and anxiously from the wings.

Trainers are the teachers of the horse show world. Their presence is ubiquitous. They are in the practice rings, they are at the in-gate, they are even in the saddle themselves. Not surprisingly, there are a good number of trainers who also ride competitively. Who are they? Some of the top names around. Grand Prix riders like Joe Fargis double as teachers of the craft.

There are different levels of training - not so much in terms of skill, but of place. There are the big-name riders who operate their own farms and, in between their own riding, school a select group of private students. There are other trainers, the majority perhaps, whose farms are more business-oriented. For these trainers, training isn't a supplemental income. It's a livelihood. Still other trainers work on farms owned by somebody else. Others are independents, "free-lancers" who travel from place to place.

The main connection between them all? Training, they say, is unbelievably time consuming. It entails daily lessons for both riders and horses. It entails matching riders with the proper horse. It entails show appearances and extended trips on

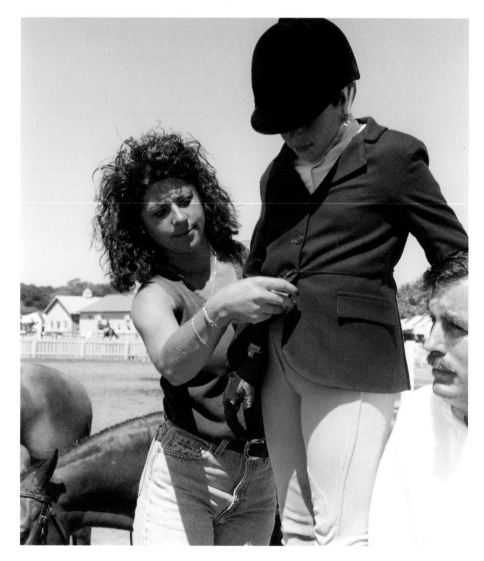

A few teachers of the trade. Opposite page: *John Lytle of Southampton's Clearview and Cheryl Reed of New York. Reed gave up full-time training because she found it too time-consuming. This page: Hamptons trainers Joe Guzman (top) and Michael Meller (bottom). Meller, it seems, has developed a few Tarkanian-like habits.*

the road. Basically, there's no need for a social calendar.

"If you're a trainer, you have no life," flatly stated New York's Cheryl Reed, who ran a stable for ten years before going into the apparently less hectic job of commercial truck sales. "It's very tough, very demanding. Forty weeks on the road. If you're a trainer you don't do anything outside of horses. You don't play tennis, you don't go to the city and see a show or anything considered normal."

"We travel, we live out of suitcases; it's not all glamorous," said Bobby Ginsberg, an independent trainer who worked out of Two Trees Stables in Bridgehampton. "A friend used to ask me: When are you going to get a real job? They don't realize that you're out there in the morning, you're out there all

Lisa Rex of Somerset Farm putting in another long, but worthwhile day.

day. By six o'clock I'm exhausted. The one thing I never see is a weekend off. That's prime riding time. Everybody wants to ride on the weekend. I love the ocean. I haven't been to the ocean in two years."

Ask any trainer about the lives they lead and you'll get answers like these. It gets pretty repetitious. "There is no social life," says Joe Guzman, an independent Hamptons trainer. That sentiment is seconded by John Lytle, who succeeded Guzman at Southampton's Clearview Farm. "It has a way of taking over your life." Not getting the drift? "We have no life," asserts Lisa Rex, who trains at her Somerset Farm on Long Island.

Now wait a minute, training can't be as all bad as that. There have to be redeeming qualities to make it worthwhile. "I do have a nice husband, so it makes it seem OK," Lisa Rex conceded. "That's the whole trick to

not minding it at all - to have someone nice to come home to at night."

What about the single trainer? Guzman says a reward of training is seeing a production through from start to finish. With new horses and riders, trainers take raw material, refine it and,

hopefully, turn it into a finished product that is a winner. "We see all phases of it, from getting the horses bathed and braided to getting in the ring," Guzman said. "It's a lot of work. You just don't show up in the ring. It's a lot of time. But when the kids do well, it makes it all worthwhile. These kids - they're like my own. They have a good trip and we're in tears. That's the reward of it: To see something you molded, this product, and see it come out well."

What's the monetary reward of training? It varies. Some get established and do well. Others roam the land and eke out what they can. Reports are decidedly mixed. Said John Lytle, "I live a comfortable lifestyle, but I don't have a lot to show for it. A lot of the people associated with horse riding are like that. Some of the top trainers are just getting by week to week."

"Somebody who freelances can make a lot of money,

East End trainer Bobby Ginsberg, still looking for that day at the beach.

if they hustle and teach a lot of lessons," said Bobby Ginsberg.

"If you do it the right way, you can make a buck," Joe Guzman said. "It takes a lot of commitment to do it right."

Most trainers like to take their act on the road and appear frequently at horse shows because that's where the top money can be made. It's also where they can establish a reputation and attract new clients. Much like gymnasts and figure skaters, when serious riders reach a certain level, they search out the best teachers to take them higher.

Consider the case of Kara Packouz. She lives in Bernardsville, N.J. She trains at Benchmark Farm. Benchmark happens to be nearly two hours away in Stamford, Ct. Yet Kara and her mother Margo Packouz will make the trip three or four times a week during the school year (summer affords extended stays) in order to work with trainer Kip Rosenthal. "We've had excellent trainers, but it's important to fit the trainer and the student," said Margo Packouz. "If you're dedicated, once you get to the point where you're really going to take it seriously, it's worth it."

It's reciprocal, because what ultimately makes training rewarding is seeing progress in students. On top of that is just a flat out love for horses. "I love it," Joe Guzman said. "I don't know how to describe it. My mom thinks I'm crazy."

"It's hard, but you know what? If I didn't love the horses I couldn't do it," said Lisa Rex. "I get paid to do something I love. Not many people can say that."

Top: *Practice, practice. Minutes in the show ring constitute but a mere fraction of a rider's total time in the saddle.* Bottom: *Margo Packouz (center) travels several hours round trip from her house in New Jersey so that her daughter Kara (right) can train with Kip Rosenthal at Benchmark Farm in Connecticut.*

The Grooms

Grooms may be the most underrated behind-the-scenes people at a horse show. It's not that riders don't appreciate them - they do - but most spectators are probably unaware of the great amount of time and energy that go into preparing horses for the show ring.

Essentially, a full day's work lies behind every ride. Before horses see the ring they have been fed, watered, exercised, bathed, brushed and braided. Grooms do this work. They do it in the obscurity of darkened stalls, leaving it to the riders to go for the glory in the spotlight of the show ring. "We put in a full day before the horses even show," claimed groom Mia Palombella. "The easy part is going and riding around the ring. The work before is the hard part - and cleaning up afterwards."

The basic day in the life of a groom starts at four or five in the morning. In the pale predawn light grooms wake the horses, give them breakfast, then take them out with a lunge line for a little morning exercise. Back at the barn, stalls await cleaning. So do the horses, who are bathed, braided and groomed after their morning workout. The whole process is reversed after show time. Typically, you'll find grooms still laboring on after sundown, undoing braids, applying poultices and wraps, preparing the stalls for the night.

Horse in hand. Grooms, whose duties keep them going from dawn to dark, are perhaps the most underrated behind-the-scenes people at a horse show.

On top of that, keep in mind that grooms who work with travelling barns are on the road for much of the year. Also

keep in mind that grooms are toward the bottom of the horse show pay scale. "The hours are long and it's a lot of hard work," said groom Eddie Gillespie. "There aren't many who like to do it."

So who does it? Many grooms you'll see at shows like the Hampton Classic are horse people who have immigrated to the U.S. from Mexico, and Ireland. Some are American kids who just like being around horses. "I can't keep an inside job," said 19-year-old Jeannie Somers of Florida's Turtle Lane Farm. "I like the horses too much."

While there are some grooms who work independently as free-lancers - Mia Palombella is an example - most

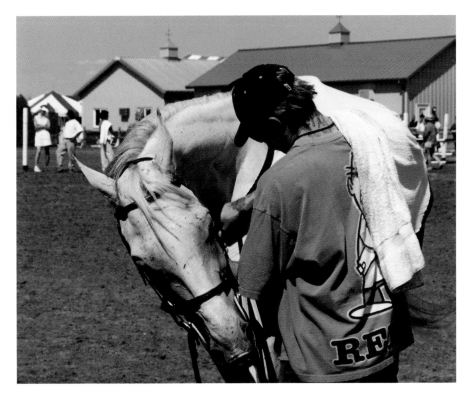

Top: *A late afternoon exercise session on the lunge line.* Bottom: *Last minute tack adjustments before show time.*

are employed by a specific farm. Gillespie, for example, works with Benchmark Farm out of Stamford, Ct. Many farms will, when they're not on the road, provide housing for their grooms. On the road, grooms either bunk with the rest of the farm at a nearby hotel or rented house, or stay in trailers right on the show grounds.

As in any profession, some grooms are valued more highly than others. Many are

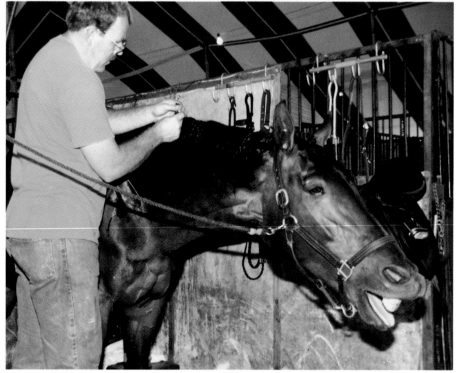

Top left: *Adrian Ford, groom and counselor at Market Street in New Jersey.* Top right: *Independent groom Mia Palombella.* Above: *Eddie Gillespie tends to a Benchmark Farm horse.* Right: *Jeanne Somers of Florida's Turtle Lane Stables.*

multitalented. Over at Anne Kursinski's Market Street Farm in Pittstown, N.J., Adrian Ford is both groom and counselor. "When we fall down Adrian has to pick us up and say how good we still are," said Market Street rider Jeanne Dupuch, who won the Calvin Klein Show Jumping Derby in 1994.

"And when everything's broken I have to fix it," Ford replied.

"Adrian's our baby-sitter, our counselor, our punching bag."

"Ha, ha, I take all the heat."

"A lot of people think of grooms as idiots," Dupuch added. "Some are. But if you have a good groom to take care of the horse it's very important. Without them, the horses don't get to the ring."

Grooming is ultra-important in show riding. Show horses have to both jump and look good. This is particularly true in the Hunter classes, where appearance counts on the scorecard.

Given the importance of grooms, you would think it must be frustrating for them to do the critical behind-the-scenes work only to stand by anonymously in a dusty practice ring while riders garner attention and glory in the green show circle. This, however, isn't necessarily so.

"For me, I like knowing that when the horses do go to the ring and people look at them, they look good," said Jeannie Somers. "When they do get a ribbon, there's personal satisfaction for me."

David Birdsall, Blacksmith

Progress has always marched a bullish path through the job market. In its wake it has left behind the traditional forms of many trades - printing, weaving, farming, to name a few. But some labors do endure in their age-old forms. One is always on display at the Hampton Classic. It is the art of the blacksmith.

Throughout its history, the Classic has been a showcase for the talents of one local farrier, David Birdsall of Water Mill. A father of three, a farm owner, Birdsall is a community guy in his trademark Southampton baseball cap. At work, Birdsall plies a trade that has remained largely unchanged over the centuries. It's all there: the hammer, the anvil, the shoes, the tongs, the leather apron. Perhaps the only difference is that today's blacksmith has the capacity, and often the need, to go mobile with great regularity. "Instead of the horse coming to the shop, the shop usually comes to the horse," Birdsall said with a wry smile.

Birdsall shoes horses at many East End farms. He also has several customers who ship him horses, which allows him to work out of his own barn. Mostly, though, Birdsall takes the forge on the road.

At each barn, Birdsall first makes it a point to learn about every horse he works on. He needs to know the capacity in which each horse is used. That will dictate how a particular horse will be shod. A horse used for nothing more than pleasure riding, for instance, can make do

Hamptons blacksmith Dave Birdsall has worked the Classic since the beginning.

with basic shoes. A big show jumper, on the other hand, would be fitted differently. He might get light aluminum shoes, or maybe additional stud holes for extra traction. A show horse also requires more frequent shoe changes, usually once a month.

You could say this is no different than fitting a person with shoes. A distance runner, after all, would not be decked out in high heels. Obviously, with

horses, there's more involved. Birdsall has got to be sure each fit is perfect, because a poor fit can damage a horse. When shod properly, a horse's foot is perfectly balanced, both front to back and side to side. When perfectly balanced, a horse's foot lands perfectly flat.

How is such perfection attained? First, the blacksmith has to take care of old business, and that's the old growth on the hoof.

Birdsall heats up a shoe, takes an imprint, then shapes to size. Birdsall says imprinting is the best way to get a perfect fit.

Out comes the file to shave it away. In essence, this is akin to trimming fingernails, except that a hoof grows a lot faster. In a month, the entire hoof will grow nearly half an inch.

Off comes this old growth. The blacksmith then takes a measurement to get an approximate fit for the new shoes. With the numbers in hand, the smith turns to the oven and heats up a shoe.

Here, the modern-day farrier diverges from his predecessors. For one thing, the typical oven is fired by butane, not coal or wood. As for the basic shoe, that can now be bought in bulk. There is no need to hammer away to build up the stock, though Birdsall can shape a straight iron bar into a basic shoe shape with a few well-placed whacks of the hammer.

Once the shoe is heated, it can be used to get a more exact measurement. Here's how. While hot, Birdsall takes the shoe and burns it into the horse's hoof. You could liken this to an orthodontist taking a mold of a patient's teeth. It may seem inhumane - when applied, the burning shoe emits a cloud of white curling smoke that smells an awful lot like burning hair. But the fact is, the horse doesn't feel it. A hoof is really nothing more than dead fingernail. Plus, a hoof is a poor conductor of heat. But just in case there is any doubt, check out the horse. You won't see him bucking madly when the red-hot shoe is applied.

By taking this burning imprint, Birdsall gets a true fit. It should be noted, though, that not all blacksmiths subscribe to the method. "A lot of people don't believe in it," Birdsall says. "They think it dries out the hoof, but the hoof is such a poor conductor of heat. If the horse felt that, I'd be a goner. I've found it's the best way to limit your mistakes. You fit the shoe to the foot, not the foot to the shoe. That's an old cliche."

After taking the imprint, Birdsall reheats the shoe and, with hammer on anvil, makes the necessary fine tunings. Once set, the shoe is nailed on. More pain and grief, it would seem, but not so. The nails are tapered. They angle out the side of the hoof. They do not drive straight in.

After that, the job is virtually done. The protruding nails are clipped off. The remaining nails, along with clips on the side, hold the shoe in place.

Sound dry and dull? Watch it some time. Watch Birdsall at the Classic. The tools, the craft are living, practical history. This isn't some Willaimsburg stage act. Another treat is watching the interplay between farrier and horse. Usually, the horse cooperates, standing quietly and lifting his hoof when asked. Yes, asked. All it usually

Birdsall, makes the rounds at East End stables with his mobile forge.

takes is a touch on the leg. "Horses, generally their disposition is really good," Birdsall noted. "They've been used by man for centuries. They'd never have been domesticated if it weren't for their disposition. Most of the time, if a horse is always a little rank it's because of no training, poor training or a misunderstanding between the handler and the horse."

Birdsall doesn't normally have "misunderstandings." But there was that one time he got booted in the calf by a horse that was "just plain mean." Horses like that, he said, often need to be tranquilized in order to be shod. That, however, is an unusual extreme. Said Birdsall, "most of the time you can snap your fingers and they'll pick the foot up for you."

A cinch, right? To watch Birdsall's deft hands work the hammer and the tongs, you'd think so. But it takes learning, naturally. There are blacksmith schools, and apprenticeships. Birdsall was home-schooled, learning a bit at the side of his father. He learned in earnest when, at the age of 22, he opened a ranch in upstate Warrensburg. Back then, Birdsall was shoeing the horses he rode. He still hits the saddle, but nowadays most of his time is devoted to the largely unchanged craft of the blacksmith.

"I always liked horses, I always wanted to be around horses," Birdsall says. "I liked the whole idea of it. I used to ride a lot. I just don't have any time for riding horses anymore. I'm always under them."

Eye on the Judges

They are the men (and women) in the booth. They are always watching. They are the ones who decide the winners in Hunter and Equitation classes. They are the judges, the people you can't have a horse show without.

Love em' or hate 'em, know this about them: Judges are all licensed and they all have to be good or horse shows like the Hampton Classic won't have them back. It's that simple. "If you aren't keeping up and doing a good job and aren't popular, you aren't going to be hired by the shows," said one judge, Bill Ellis of Ocala Florida, as he scored the Children's Hunter Classic with Don Stewart Jr. at the 1994 Hampton Classic.

All show judges are licensed by the American Horse Shows Association. Judges enter at the ground floor and work their way up. Prospective judges start out doing small shows. If they're proficient, they will get a "small r." That stands for recording status, and it allows judges to work recognized events, though mostly small ones. Once they have their "big R," or recorded status, judges are qualified to work top A-rated shows like the Hampton Classic. Just what the judges will be judging is up to them. Judges must apply for the specific events they want to grade.

Who is the prototypical judge? Someone from the show riding business, perhaps a trainer or a former rider. Previous experience, though, does not always make for a quality judge. "Usually, most judges have been trainers or riders themselves," said Jimmy Toon of Purchase, New York, who is both a trainer and a judge. "You would think someone who's active in the business would be a good judge, but judging separates itself. If you don't do a good job, you don't get asked back."

Judges make decent wages. The standard rate is $300 a day, with all expenses paid. Their days are long, though, as they watch competition and score it from morning to late afternoon. It would seem all the watching would get tedious after a while. Judges, though, say they can stay focused. Then again, they have to. "It's like anything else," said Bill Ellis. "Once you do it enough it's just part of the duty. And during the day you usually get to rest. Even during the competition, if some horse isn't so competitive, you can take a mental break. And when you judge shows of this caliber, it's still exciting. You stay up for it."

While they are theoretically detached and neutral observers, judges are not islands in the horse stream. They personally know many of the riders, many of the horses. They know how they perform. That knowledge, though, has to be put aside when it's time to score.

"We know a lot of the horses, but still have to judge their performance," Ellis noted. "Otherwise, if it was just a case of knowing the horse and knowing how it performs, you wouldn't have to judge. You could line them up and give them ribbons. It's a competition-based performance. Because it's subjective there can be some discrepancies. But I feel most of the judges try to do a good job."

What are judges looking for in the Hunter and Equitation events? Style and grace, basically. They want to see harmony between horse and rider. "We want to see a good mover, a good jumper," Jimmy Toon elaborated. "It's like when you go to a nightclub and watch couples dance. You pick out the couple that moves well together. Riding is a couple. It's two people - well, it's an animal and a human being. The team that performs the best together should be the winner."

Of course, just who was best is an issue occasionally disputed. Like their umpire and referee brethren, show riding judges will be questioned from time to time. Not everyone is always happy with the final call. But here's a reminder: From his vantage point, the judge will see what others may not. And in competition ridden

Judge Bill Ellis

on the flat, in which there are numerous riders in the ring, a judge cannot see everyone at all times.

"People will say they don't like the judge, but in that spot where they're sitting things look differently from what they do at the ingate," Toon stated. "So you don't need to throw the blame at the judge. Everybody should do some judging. It makes for a better horizon."

Toon has followed his own advice. A trainer by trade, Toon said judging has given him a valuable perspective to take back into the ring. "As a trainer, teacher and rider, it's helped me," he said. "Sitting on that side of the ring has increased my knowledge."

Chapter VIII: Super Sunday

Grand Prix Sunday

The show has already been in town for nearly a week. For six days, morning to dusk, the riding has gone down in the show rings, in the practice rings. A seemingly endless parade of riding caps and numbers has ridden by. The crowds have come in, watch ,spent, consumed, and departed. All the tramping of feet and hooves has carved worn dusty paths into what was a lush green expanse.

It's odd. Even at a show of the Hampton Classic's stature, a sense of weariness, of finality has set in by Saturday night, especially if you've been roaming the grounds all week. You leave with the setting sun, passing by the trailers and the stables and the pickup trucks unloading hay thinking how sweet it would be to sleep in the next morning. But you can't. One day remains, and it is the biggest of the week. Somehow, the energy has to be dredged up for one last round, for Grand Prix Sunday.

The curtain opens and, as enjoyable as the week has been, it all seems to be a prelude to what comes on that second Sunday. The crowds haven't so much doubled and tripled. They seem to have multiplied and divided. The media is suddenly out in full force. The local sports people and the daily writers, have been here all week. But now the horse mags are in, the society pubs, too. They're all here to catch a piece of the action in the Grand Prix Tent, because today is the day the stars come out to play. Even the local patrons are decked

Fan attendance, course design, prize winnings and all other elements hit their peak on Grand Prix Sunday. So does the riding. Opposite: *Grand Prix rider Michael Endicott.*

out. Polo shirts have been exchanged for ties and blazers.

Perhaps you know a friend or have a pass. You go in and you are immediately washed up in a sea of hobnobbers and handshakers, hustling caterers, champagne bottles and food-laden tables. The air is, as Grand Prix Tent host Michael Braverman will tell you, electric. A camera crew nabs Peter Jennings, looking sharp in shades and a shirt opened at the neck. A paparazzi swarm hones in on Susan Lucci as if she were honey coated. She is seated, eating lunch. She smiles, electric white. The popping flashes are hardly brighter. Want your 15 minutes of fame? Have a buddy take your photo under this tent on Grand Prix Day and watch the cameras descend.

You duck, dodge and shimmy your way onward, moving along familiar ground past the people who have been here all week: The local stables, rid-

ers, trainers. You recognize them, but they look, feel different. Peter Boyle has been around virtually every day with no more presence than any other father on hand to watch his kid ride. Today he is unequivocally Peter Boyle, actor. It must be something in the air. Something that rubs off when you pass those heavily guarded gates.

It's that dream state, you

know? You look around. The tents, the ropes, the white chairs, the suggestive eyes of the overhead Harper's Bazaar posters: They're all the same, just like they were Tuesday and Thursday and all the other days.

But, clearly, this is a different place, and if you're claustrophobic or shy, it's not for you. There is no hiding here, no quiet place to retreat. What they say about this

Grand Prix Tent is true. It is electric. And with that great big yellow and white tent overhead, none of the electricity can escape. It just swirls around and feeds upon itself, growing stronger.

If you don't have a pass, the security guards have found you by now and it's out you go. No threats, no jostling. Just "our friend here will be leaving us now." Perhaps you see Agneta Currey, the chairwoman, coming in as you are being escorted out. Her hair has been done, she's got on her heels. She looks good, always does, but you want to tell her she was absolutely flawless when she was in the ring at sunset, laboring over the jumps and the decorations with Conrad Homfeld and his crew long after all the crowds had gone away. As she comes in now you know she's already been here and back. You know that at 7 o'clock that morning she was out in that ring, planting more flowers, helping arrange the pumpkins and apples that now dress the Grand Prix ring.

The ring, of course, looks magnificent. The jumps are all the same, but today they have a greater aura. It must be all the decorations, brought forth in one last splurge of supply and labor.

It must be the full stands, too. Both bleachers are jam-packed. You can hardly move. The crowd, it is said, numbers 20,000. They are here to see the big show, the $100,000 Crown Royal Grand Prix. The number doesn't register with you, perhaps. The whole show is so big, so special it just seems to be another superlative. Then you think a bit and realize that one of those Grand Prix riders now walking the course

Alan Keedy, Ringmaster

The crowds are packed in, the banners are flying and the Grand Prix ring stands ready for the big event: the Hampton Classic's $100,000 Crown Royal Grand Prix. There will be no riding, though, until the ringmaster sounds his horn.

At the Classic, the ringmaster is Alan Keedy of Coker Farms in Bedford, New York. You can't miss him. He's the guy decked out in full coachman's livery: beaver skin top hat, red livery coat (complete with brass buttons), white breeches, tan leggings and paddock boots. In case all that somehow passes you by, you're sure to note the slender 52-inch coachman's horn Keedy sounds to summon riders to the ring.

With his horn and uniform, Keedy is a living embodiment of the old English coachman's tradition (he even has a genuine fare bag and time-

piece). Back in the days of the travelling horse-pulled coach, coachmen would carry horns for both safety and entertainment purposes. Horns were used as a warning device. While pulling into a town, coachmen would sound their call to alert pedestrians and other coaches. Because of the horn's long, slender design, the calls could be heard over long distances. The horns would also be used in between towns, when the coachman would play tunes to entertain the passengers.

The songs Keedy plays at the Hampton Classic on Grand Prix Day are all coach originals. "Silby's Favorite," a song once played to passengers between towns, is sounded before the CK Equitation Classic. To summon the Grand Prix riders, Keedy brings out "Olde Time's Chorus." The lively "Tootler" precedes the jump off. To close the show, Keedy sounds "Taps."

Keedy started playing the coachman's horn while working at a farm in Michigan. The owner of the farm was interested in finding a player. Keedy, a clarinet player in high school, volunteered. He was given a tape of coach songs and learned to play by ear.

Keedy eventually made his way to Judy Richter's Coker Farm in New York. She put him in touch with organizers at the Classic, who hired the hornman for the 1991 show. Keedy volunteered that first year. Classic organizers liked him so much they brought him back, this time for pay. Keedy has been a Classic staple since. Keedy's work at the Classic has also earned him jobs at other shows.

A rider himself, Keedy appreciates the chance to lend a traditional air to the show jumping world. It also puts him in the middle of the action. As ringmaster, Keedy not only sounds the call, he's also responsible for issuing the ribbons at show's end. "This is a way for me to be a part of the sport and I love it dearly," said Keedy, who competes as an Adult Amateur Jumper. "It's very satisfying to be out here in the ring and to do my part to keep this a tradition."

Grand Prix History

The Hampton Classic Grand Prix has grown in stature and payoff. What started as a $10,000 event has ballooned tenfold to $100,000 - one of the highest Grand Prix payoffs in the country.

The drama has matched the price tag. There have been jump-offs in every year but one. There have been grand prix decided on the last ride of the day. There has even been a Grand Prix won by a rider who had survived an airplane crash less than two weeks before. That was Michael Matz, who may have maxed out the drama meter with his winning ride in 1989. But each year has had its moment.

The Hampton Classic's first official Grand Prix winner was Bernie Traurig and "Southside." The year was 1977, the show's first as the Hampton Classic.

In 1978, Classic fans saw the aptly named Lynn Little pull out victory with "Port." The five-foot-two Little was a jockey who had taught herself and Port, a former English racehorse, how to jump. She won by three-tenths of a second on the last ride of a three-horse jump-off.

The rider beaten out by Little, Mark Jungherr, returned in 1979 to win with "Just Plain Wilbur." For a second straight year, fans were treated to Grand Prix won on the day's last ride. Jungherr won a nine-horse jumpoff with two seconds to spare.

The 1980 Grand Prix saw the price tag rise from $10,000 to $15,000. For champion Melanie Smith, winning the Grand Prix with "Calypso" by a slim two-tenths of a second brought another bonus. It qualified the rider for the World Cup.

It was Grand Prix veteran Rodney Jenkins' turn to rise to the top in 1981 with "Idle Dice." At the time, the 18-year-old horse was the biggest money winner in Open Jumper history. It would eventually become the first horse inducted into the Show Jumping Hall of Fame. For Jenkins, the win was the first of three he would post at the Hampton Classic Grand Prix.

A footnote to the 1981 event: The runner-up was local legend Harry deLeyer of East Hampton. It was the third straight second-place finish for deLeyer at the Classic. He rode the Grand Prix course cleanly for three straight years, yet never won the event.

The 1982 Grand Prix ushered in the wave of the future. It was the first held at the Classic's new home in Bridgehampton and it was won by Conrad Homfeld, who would later become the Classic's Grand Prix course designer.

In 1982, Homfeld was still riding full-time. He was two years away from a silver medal at the 1984 Olympics. The horse he rode to victory at the Classic, "Touch of Class," would win Olympic gold with Homfeld's partner, Joe Fargis. Had he not been recovering from a broken leg, Fargis would have rode Touch of Class at the 1982 Classic. Homfeld was just filling in. Using shortened strides, he beat favorite Katie Monahan, who had four of the 13 horses in the jumpoff.

Rodney Jenkins would own the winner's circle for the next two years. He won in 1983 with "Coastline" to capture his 50th overall Grand Prix victory. In 1984, he beat Ann Kursinski in a two-horse jumpoff with "Sugar Ray." Victory was indeed sweet. No other rider has won three Grand Prix at the Classic.

After the repeat by Jenkins, the Classic would see different Grand Prix winners in each of the next four years. In 1985, the "Year of the Mud," Anthony D'Ambrosio won aboard "Nimmedor," a four year old in only its second year of showing. In 1986, the first year the Classic used a qualifying event to winnow out the Grand Prix field, Katharine Burdsall and "The Natural" beat back Rodney Jenkins' bid for a fourth title. The 1987 Grand Prix and its rain-slicked course belonged to Jay Land and the aptly named "Leapy Lad." Then, in 1988, Katie Monahan made up for her missed opportunity six years earlier by winning with "The Empress." That 1988 Classic had the added prestige of being the final qualifier for the 1988 U.S. Olympics. Joe Fargis led the list of qualifiers.

By now, the Grand Prix purse was up to $50,000. What it gained in 1989 in terms of emotion and drama was even more valuable. That was the year Michael Matz survived an airline crash that killed more than 100 passengers in Iowa. Just 11 days after the tragedy, in which he was credited with saving the lives of two children, Matz strode into the Hampton Classic Grand Prix ring and followed up a hero's welcome with a winning performance aboard "Schnapps."

Matz returned in 1990 to win with "Heisman." Matz won by being the only rider to go clean in the first round. It was the first and only Classic Grand Prix to date that did not feature a jump-off. A tricky quadruple combination at the end of a tough Homfeld course was the culprit.

In 1991, a famous local rider attained a major prize that had previously eluded him. That was Joe Fargis of Southampton. Amid his Olympic medals and international titles and other Grand Prix victories, Fargis had never won at the Classic. That changed in 1991 when Fargis rode to the top aboard "Mill Pearl," the horse with whom he had won a silver at the 1988 Olympics.

In 1992, chronic second-fiddle Jeffrey Welles, he of the six second-place finishes in 1989, tasted glory with "Serengeti." The following year, Beezie Patton and "Ping Pong" won on the penultimate ride of the jump-off.

Welles was back in the winner's circle in 1994, and in dramatic fashion. Just minutes after being thrown by Serengeti in the jump-off, Welles rebounded to win on the last ride of the day with a springy thoroughbred by the name of "Irish." The last-second victory - make that two-tenths of a second victory - denied a third title to Michael Matz, who was sitting pretty in both first and second heading into the final round. But like Matz and all the pros know, you don't sit comfortably until the last horse rides, especially on Grand Prix Day.

Joe Fargis competes in the 1994 Grand Prix with Mill Pearl. Fargis and Mill Pearl won the Grand Prix in 1991.

decked in a spiffy blazer and white breeches, is going to walk out of here with $33,000, maybe even more, just for riding a horse. It has to be a perfect ride, though. The one that, at the end of the day, is faster than all the others, the one that leaves no rail lying on the field.

Presently, the ringmaster sounds his horn. Olde Time's Chorus: The call to ride. The first name is announced and the riding begins. The crowd silences for each ride, watching intently, sighing with each knockdown. On the clean rounds a murmur rises as horse and rider work deeper into the course. The murmur builds to a low roar on the final jumps. When the last is cleared, the place erupts. The fans love Fargis, they love Matz. They also love every clean ride.

The contest moves on to the jump off. Only the best on this day remain. It's been a long afternoon. Perhaps the crowd is getting a little sleepy. Perhaps, but the best still lies ahead. The course has been shortened; the time reduced. Riders are pushing their horses faster. Corners are taken tighter. The approach to jumps is drastically shorter, yet still these amazing horses manage to get up and over. Hoof hits rail. Maybe it falls, maybe it just wobbles and stays in place. The crowd oohs and aahs and erupts once more. Someone has set the pace. Maybe someone follows and breaks it. Maybe someone with even more daring and a little more luck is still waiting in the wings. Maybe it will all come down to the very last ride, a feverish, last-second dash to the finish. What could be better? Nothing here. Not on this day. It is Grand Prix Sunday. It is meant to be the best.

Epilogue

Denouement

There is one drawback to the Hampton Classic: Its ending. All things must end, of course. But the Classic comes to an all too sudden, almost jarring close. Once the Grand Prix is done, once the winner has received the blue ribbon and has led the victory parade out of the ring, the show starts to come down. Workers are removing rails and jump standards even while the press is peppering the day's winner with questions.

The crowds have filtered out, merging into the slow drive home. By the time they get there, the Grand Prix ring will have been undone, all the television cables brought down and coiled. Over at the stables, what farms remain are busy loading their horses onto trailers. It is not yet dusk, but it should be. Everything has that coming-down feel. It's not just the end of the show, really. It's the end of the summer.

"It's so sad," said Maureen Matthews, the Southampton florist who labored before and during the show on Grand Prix decoration. "It's hard to imagine something that took so long to set up is over, and with such suddenness."

It's true. Within days all the tents, stables, bleachers, tables, chairs and fences will be taken down and away. They are brought down quickly, but not with the same zest with which

The Classic breakdown begins as soon as the Grand Prix ends. In the ring, jumps are dismantled. Out on Pleasant Alley, tack and other stable gear are packed up and on-loaded along with the horses for the drive back home.

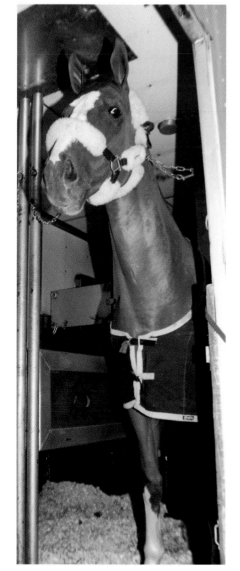

they went up. The energy that carried workers up to the Classic and through the week has pretty much left town with the show. "You want to see morale at its lowest come back the Monday after the show," said Neil O'Connor, the grounds coordinator. "The show's over and you don't even realize it's over. A lot of people don't show up. It's too depressing. You're going, going, going then, Sunday evening, boom."

Boom, then nothing. It's like the day after Christmas. All the presents have been opened, and while the gifts were nice, there remains that empty feeling that follows the passing of anything so eagerly anticipated.

Still, the show must go on. It is over, of course, but Classic business remains. Billings and collections must be attended to. At the organizational level, the Board of Directors gets together and starts planning for next year. "It's the best time to remember what went wrong," explained Agneta Currey.

Outside, Bud Topping turns his attention back to the grounds. All those acres that were so full and green when the show started are now chewed up pretty good. All of it must be reseeded.

It is nearly two weeks since the show ended. It is still warm out, but fall is unmistakably on its way. Bud drives his tractor across open, lonely fields. The Hunter rings don't seem too empty. Thanks to the hedges that have been planted over the years there is definition, a sense of what has been there and what will return.

Till We Meet Again: Bud Topping commences the work that completes one show and starts another.

Permanent plantings also remain in the Grand Prix ring. But with the tents and grandstands down, the place looks forlorn. In this state, the magic green ring is just another field. The ground upon which the stabling tents stood is the emptiest of all. There is no grass remaining, just one giant dirt spot. It's as if a forest fire blew through.

For Bud, it's not so bad. The seed is going down. The grounds, on their way to recovery, start to blend back in with their natural surroundings now that all the tents and people have gone away. "It's nice now," Bud says. "The geese go cutting across. There were two deer up here yesterday, some foxes, too."

Yes. Now that the show has come and gone, the old inhabitants return. Bud starts the tractor back up and resumes seeding. The seed will burrow into the ground through winter, emerge in spring and grow again, turning full and green just as another Classic arrives in late summer. So the cycle is sure to play out just as it has for 20 years.

Twenty years: It is an anniversary of distinction, and yet the show is still so relatively young. There will be more years, more decades.

What do they hold in store for a show that is already at the top? Where does the show go from here? Bigger doesn't seem to be the answer. There simply isn't any more space. The solution? "We have all the horses we can handle, we have all the tables filled," said Agneta Currey. "So the only way we can grow now is by doing everything better."

Better: It's been the Classic's watchword for 20 years. There is no point in changing the vocabulary now.

Overleaf: *The Wake of the Show. Photo courtesy David Lynch & Eastern Aerial Photography.*

Acknowledgments

The time has come to hang up the saddle and close the stable door. Before heading out, I need to issue the appropriate thank yous. I am much obliged to Tony Hitchcock, Jean Lindgren and the Hampton Classic staff for their time and co-operation, which were always available. I would also like to single out Classic Chairwoman Agneta Currey, who, without having to say a word, made me see just why the Hampton Classic has been a successful show. I must also tip my hat twice to Diana De Rosa, the press officer. This book's title, with a slight prepositional alteration, was suggested and graciously lent by her. She was also a prime contact and a wealth of information. Thanks also to all those who allowed themselves to be interviewed and/or photographed, in particular Patsy Topping and Conrad Homfeld. Thanks to Jean Raymond and Susan Addes for proof reading.

As for a dedication, that is easy. If it weren't for my wife Helen, this book would have lacked the necessary quality photography. I did take many of the pictures. She took the best ones, including the cover shot. Also , thanks to David Lynch and Eastern Aerial Photography for donating the "before, during and after" aerial shots of the showgrounds. Thanks to Larry Trachtenbroit and Hampton Bays Photo for developing and enlarging our work. Thanks to Maxine Mortensen and Karen O'Neill for sales support.

The Classic Experience was published by my partner Carl W. Miller. He suggested the idea one evening on the back porch, noting the lack of any previous publication on the show. Combining his publishing contacts with my reporting, we have produced a work that we hope will fill that void. Thanks to Susan Miller, his wife, for taking care of loose ends, marketing and sales support, and helping Carl to bring this project to completion.

Of course, we must thank our families and friends. Thanks to our daughter Tessa for her patience during this project. Thanks to R.E.M. for putting out a new album to get me through deadline.

BC

THE 1989 HAMPTON CLASSIC
SNAKE HOLLOW ROAD · BRIDGEHAMPTON · NEW YORK
JULY 23–30

THE HAMPTON CLASSIC
JULY 22 – JULY 29, 1990
SNAKE HOLLOW ROAD BRIDGEHAMPTON NEW YORK

THE HAMPTON CLASSIC
AUGUST 23-30, 1992 SNAKE HOLLOW ROAD, BRIDGEHAMPTON, NEW YORK